*A New Ham I Am! *
Made Simple for Cruisers

1st Edition

Handbook for
Starting the Dream
Volume VI

By Commander T. L. Sparks
US Navy, Retired

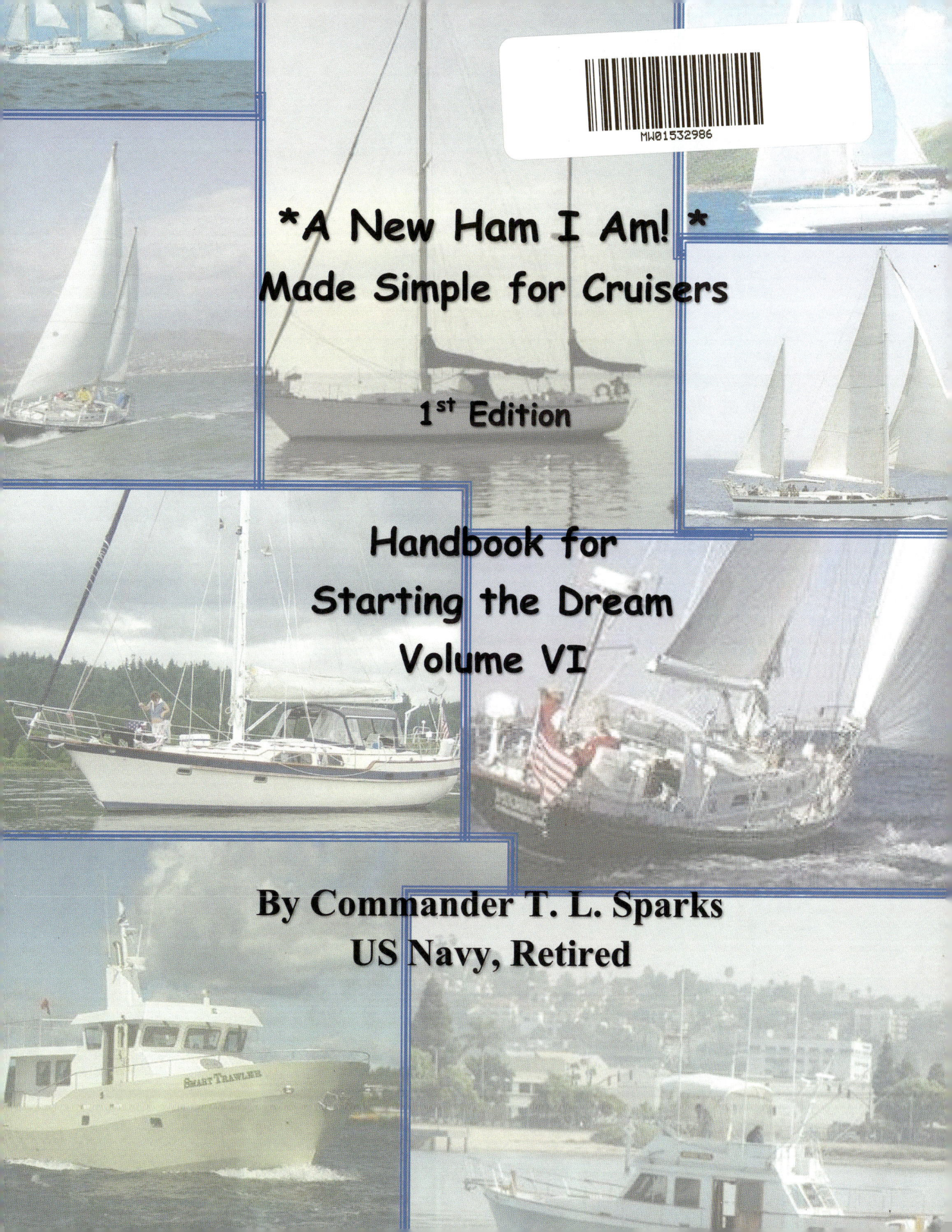

Dedication and Special Thanks

Joe on S/V Valparaiso told me the same story I have been hearing for years. He said, "I took a Ham course and that was a waste of time. The instructors just told us a lot of stories. I used a book and some on-line studying to get my General class license, but no one told me what to do with my radio."

So this book is for you Joe and the other new Hams that need the same help!

Special Thanks goes to: Elizabeth on S/V Vivacia; Gysi of Princess Del Mar; Carolyn, TheBoatGalley.com; and Rick S/V La Vita for identifying items to be covered within this book.

For all the help with the initial editing, a many thanks to Fran on S/V Red and my wife Patricia on S/V Sunnyside.

The "A New Ham I Am – Made Simple for Cruiser" final review was completed by Captain Ron on the S/V Boundless and Joe on S/V Valparaiso.

Many thinks to all that contributed to make this book useful for a Cruiser that has also become a Ham.

Foreword

The purpose of this book is to help New Hams bridge the gap between getting a license and using the license. There are two different types of Hams. There are "Hams who go Cruising and Cruisers who become Hams."

A frequent comment by cruisers who become Hams is: *"Now that I have a Ham License, I don't know what to do with it. The (course, books, or questions on line) did not teach me anything about operating my radio."*

Cruisers that become Hams will use High Frequency Single Sideband (HF SSB) radios as a cruising tool and not typically as a Ham station. HF SSB radios provide a method for cruisers to communicate with other cruisers, get information and do email away from port. In an emergency HF SSB is probably the best tool to actually get help.

HF SSB communications nets provide excellent practice in using and understanding the anomalies of HF SSB radio. Being a part of the nets also allows you to get to know other cruisers even if you have never met them. Cruisers are frequently in foreign countries, may not speak the local language, understand the culture, or laws. If you need help getting to know other cruisers in your area can be really important. If you are cruising you *will* need help at some time.

HF SSB allows you to know other people before you need them.

While the static on HF SSB often wears on people, being able to talk to a friend on a long passage can be the perfect solution to a long day. Talking to friends can actually make it seem as though the static has disappeared.

When you have a Ham License, you become the "resident radio expert". As a result, this book also contains some of the basics for using the Marine Band frequencies including methods of **calling for help in an emergency.**

Some basic information on getting the licenses you need to cruise has also been included.

About the Author

Terry Sparks Naval career started as an electronics technician repairing communications, radar, computer and satellite tracking equipment. He served at communications stations, on two submarines, and one satellite tracking and injection facility.

After leaving active duty he joined the Naval Reserves went back to college and attained a Bachelor of Science degree in Electrical Engineering. Around the 15 year point in Navy Reserve career, Terry was promoted to Ensign and ultimately retired as a Commander after 33.5 years total service.

Terry's civilian positions have included: Chief Engineer KVEW television; Electronics Instructor for Columbia Basin College; and Systems Engineer and Engineering and Software Development manager for Westinghouse, Combustion Engineering, and ABB Inc. Terry also retired from ABB Inc. in 2008 after twenty years and went cruising.

You can also follow our cruising adventure at our web page and find out where we are today at: http://sunnyside-adventure.webs.com

Table of Contents

Licenses

1. Cruising Communications Licenses Needs

The best time to start thinking about what communications you need for the cruising the world on your boat is when you are still in your home port.

Many cruisers leave home without a Ham license and some without even a Ships Station License. Later they find out how much they lose out on by not having a Ham license and without a Ships Station License they are actually operating the transmitting equipment illegally in other countries.   Now while cruising, they struggle to get a Ships Station License and a General Class Ham License.   Chapter one in this book provides some help on how to get a Ham license.

Some people planning on going cruising do get their Ham License, but have no idea why it is something they need.

After a Cruiser obtains a Ham license, the next question is: "What can I do with the license?"

This book is intended to help a new Ham get started being a Ham operator while cruising and to allow him/her to get the most out of the new Ham license.

Ships Station License Requirement

While the focus of this book is what to do with a Ham license, it is important that a cruiser also have a Ships Station License.   This license covers all the marine transmitting equipment on your boat. E.g. Marine VHF radio, Radar, EPIRB, and the HF SSB radio on Marine assigned frequencies including the ITU channels.

In all countries, installing Marine High Frequency Single Sideband (HF SSB) radio requires some form of ships station license.   This license will then typically cover all transmitting equipment on your boat.

Even if you do not have HF SSB equipment on your boat, departing your country or even just talking to vessels from another country requires a Ships Station License.

Why Get a Ham License to go Cruising?

Hams that go cruising already have a good idea why a Ham license is important, but what about a cruiser that gets a Ham license?

The Social Aspect
- You will be spending a lot of time on your boat alone or with another party. The nets give you someone else to talk with.
- With a Ham license you can make calls home for free via other hams that are shore based.
- Other cruisers will become your closest support and friends, so you will want to stay in touch with them.

Help
- Hams all over the world help each other it is like a mission in life.
- You can get weather, health, repair assistance etc. by calling on other hams.
- Since the other cruisers that are hams are your friends, they will clearly help you if you have a boat emergency.

Getting a Ham License

Ham Licenses in most countries come with different levels. In the United States there are three levels: Technician; General; and Amateur Extra. As you get a higher class license, you get to use more frequencies.

While a Ham license is not required for cruising, a Ham license is a giant step in the right direction for safety at sea.

In the US a General class license allows use of HF SSB Ham frequencies which are used by cruisers every day. A General class license also allows you to use HF SSB Winlink email for free, get weather information, and even text another boat.

Regardless what country you are starting from, make sure your Ham license allows transmission on bands within the frequencies ranging from 2MHz to 29.9MHz.

2. Getting an Amateur (Ham) License

While the purpose of this book is to help a new Ham get started, it is worth spending a few paragraphs on how to get a Ham License.

As a side note, if you do not have a Ships Station license for your boat, you should consider getting the Ships Station License prior to even working on your Ham license. See Appendix V.

The Appendixes in this book also include valuable information for both Ham and the Marine side of your High Frequency Single Sideband (HF SSB) transceiver.

Ham Licenses are country specific. The best place to meet your countries requirements for a Ham License is in your home country. There may be other options to obtain the Ham license, but it may be much more difficult in another country if it is even possible to get a Ham license outside your country.

Getting a US Ham License

To get a US Ham License you must have an address in the US. In other words, you do not have to be a citizen of the United States to obtain a US Ham License.

Locations
It is easy to find a location to complete the testing and become a US Ham. There are many locations that give the test across the US and the frequency of testing in some cases is as often as every Saturday morning in the San Diego, CA area. In smaller communities it may only be once a year given by a Ham Club after a training class.

Getting Ready for the Ham Test
There are many training options available to cruisers to help them prepare to take and pass a Ham test. Since the Ham License no longer requires Morse code testing, it is much easier for everyone to pass the test and obtain a General class Ham license.

Training Classes
There are many classes put on by Hams and Ham clubs to help beginners learn the fundamentals to become a Ham. If you would like to attend a formal training class you can find one by going to the ARRL site and searching for a class in your area.

At the end of the class the Ham test associated with the level of the training class are frequently given.

<u>Training for a Ham Test</u>
There are many books available for training that may be found on-line or at your local Ham store.   There are big differences in the books however.

Some of the books contain the entire recent bank of test questions used for the Ham tests.   This book is basically used to help you memorize the answers to the test questions. The books are typically used by folks who just want to get a license that allows them to use the frequencies. This is the case with most cruisers.

The next level of book contains training on each subject with sample tests in the back of the book. An example of these books would be "the ARRL Ham Radio License Manual". There is one book for each exam level. The book now contains a practice exam CD.   In most cases these books are used by folks who have a basic understanding of communications and electronics and hope to become a real Ham.

<u>On-Line Training</u>
On-line internet training has become the easiest way for everyone to prepare for a Ham test. There are sample tests given at several internet locations. A few are listed below. The web sites may be used for free.   The sites utilize the present question banks to generate sample tests. When you can pass the online tests with a score of 90% or better, you are probably ready to take the real test.

The Test
To obtain the Technician and General Class license you must get twenty-six (26) of the thirty-five (35) multiple choice questions correct.   For the Amateur Extra test you must get thirty-seven (37) of the fifty (50) multiple choose questions correct.   The questions are drawn from a bank of questions that are updated every few years.

Links to Training and Testing

To help you find an exam location, go to this ARRL web page and search for exams in your area.   http://www.arrl.org/exam_sessions/search

Another good source for tests is to contact your local Ham club.   One way to find a club in your area is to click on your state at this web site.
http://www.Hamdepot.com/

If you are already Cruising and now realize you need a Ham License, it is still possible. For West Coast Cruisers the Ham exams are given occasionally in La Paz, BCS and Nuevo Vallarta, JAL Mexico.   The tests are given at Club Cruceros and at the Vallarta Yacht Club respectively so check their web sites for the latest exam information.
http://www.clubcruceros.net/ & http://www.vallartayachtclub.org/

Training Classes
http://www.arrl.org/find-an-amateur-radio-license-class

Online Practice Tests
http://aa9pw.com/radio/ , http://www.eHam.net/exams/ , http://www.w8mhb.com/ , and http://www.qrz.com/ht/

Other Options

This site has links to various forms of training including free, Amazon Kindle, Barnes and Nobel Nook and printed versions.
http://www.kb6nu.com/tech-manual/

So bottom line there is lots of training available for preparing you to take the test and most of it is free.

Getting a Canadian Ham License

While I am not from Canada, there is a lot of information on-line to help Canadians get a license. Canada only has two levels of Ham licenses, Basic and Advanced. But they also allow HF use by applicants who do well on the examination and/or are certified to have basic level qualifications as a CW operator. (Morse code use)

Frequency assignments within Canada are assigned as follows:
1. Amateur Operators Certificate with Basic Qualification
2. Amateur Operators Certificate with Basic Qualification "with Honors" (where the holder achieved 80% or higher on the examination
3. An Amateur Operators Certificate with Basic Qualification and Morse Code (5 w.p.m.) Qualification
4. Amateur Operators Certificate with Basic and Advanced Qualification
5. On some frequency bands, Hams are secondary users. Within the shared bands, Hams may not cause interference to the primary users.

The Basic exam is composed of one hundred (100) questions and you must get at least seventy (70) questions correct to pass.

For the Advanced license you must get thirty-five (35) of the fifty (50) questions correct.

Information on how to obtain a Ham license in Canada can be found at the following web sites.

Canadian Web site links

General Information
https://www.rac.ca/en/amateur-radio/beginner-info/
http://www.ic.gc.ca/eic/site/smt-gst.nsf/eng/h_sf01709.html
http://www.ic.gc.ca/eic/site/smt-gst.nsf/eng/sf08435.html

Training Courses and Study Guides to Help Get the License
http://www.Hamradiolicenseexam.com/faq.htm
https://www.rac.ca/store/catalogue_e.php

Practice Exams in French and English

https://www.rac.ca/en/amateur-radio/beginner-info/exHaminer/

A study guides are also available on-line for free.
http://studyguide.eqth.info/ and http://www.Hamelmer.com/

You can also download the recent question pool at the ARRL web site.
http://www.arrl.org/question-pools

There are also on-line training classes that may be purchased.
http://www.Hamradiolicenseexam.com/index.html

Ham License in Other Countries
While the International Telecommunications Union (ITU) in general controls all the frequencies in the world, the frequency allocations and licensing processes are controlled by the country providing the actual Amateur License.

The Basics

3. HF SSB Basics

Questions Cruisers Ask About HF SSB

HF vs. SSB

The first confusion is over the miss-interpretation that High Frequency (HF) radio is Amateur/Ham radio and Single Sideband (SSB) radio is Marine radio or often vice versa. This is usually the result of a confused cruiser telling a new cruiser all about HF SSB radio.   HF vs. SSB is an easy question to answer.

HF radio and SSB are both Marine and Amateur radio.   HF (High Frequency band) is the frequency range used and SSB (Single Side Band) is the type of modulation or in other words, how the voice (intelligence) is applied to the HF band frequency being transmitted and received.

The lower end of most Marine radios is typically the upper end of the Medium Frequency or MF band.   The MF frequency band is 300 KHz to 3MHz and the HF frequency band is 3 to 30 MHz.   So, marine radios actually include a portion of the MF frequency band as well as most of the HF frequency band.

The legal use of the frequencies on your marine radio is dependent on the licenses held by the boat and the people on the boat.

One minor difference in Marine radio and Ham radio is that Marine HF SSB uses all Upper Sideband (USB) and Amateur radio typically uses Lower Sideband (LSB) for the lower frequencies and USB in the higher frequencies.

I Cannot Hear Anyone

Another statement frequently made by new HF SSB operators is, *"I have tuned the radio all over and I do not hear anyone, it must not be working"*.

The issue here is that the typical HF SSB radio covers all the frequencies between approximately 1.6 Million Cycles per second (2MHz) to thirty million cycles per second (30MHz) in three thousand cycles per second (3KHz) steps.   If we count the possible steps we find that (30,000,000 – 1,600,000)/3,000 is over 9466 possible channels.   While the majority of these frequencies are assigned to other radio services such as government, aircraft, military, etc., there are still many frequencies assigned to marine and Ham operators.

Bottom line, there is no channel 16, as on marine VHF radio, to find other boats. You need to have a plan or Digital Selective Calling for HF SSB communications. However, in an emergency there are designated frequencies that you can contact search and rescue (SAR) groups around the world.. Communications planning will be discussed later in this book.

All I Hear is Static
The most common complaint by new HF SSB operators is about noise. *"All I here is static."* HF SSB radio can be noisy. Some new Hams say the static really wears on them. A new Ham recently told me that now that she is using the radio and knows people on the other end (at least their voice on the radio), the static seems to disappear. While I never thought about that before, it does seem true.

HF SSB modulation is similar to the modulation on the AM side of the radio in your car. SSB is a really a form of Amplitude Modulation (AM) and as such, typically picks up surrounding noise. That is why we listen to music on the Frequency Modulated (FM) radio in our cars.

Marine VHF, like the FM radio in our cars, is impacted minimally by electric noise. Below is a look at how AM radio transmits a single 2,000Hz (2 KHz) tone signal at 100% modulation. See Appendix

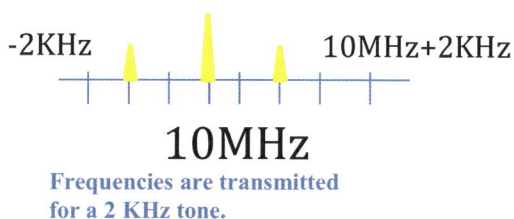

-2KHz   10MHz+2KHz

10MHz

Frequencies are transmitted for a 2 KHz tone.

AM Signal with 2KHz 100% Modulation

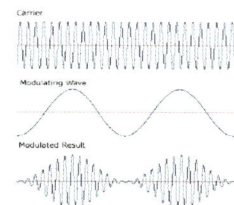

For the AM signal, the frequencies being transmitted include the 10 MHz we call the carrier frequency as well as the sideband frequencies of 10.002MHz and 9.998MHz. The tone modulating the 10 MHz creates both the upper and lower sidebands. Transmitting the 10 MHZ carrier frequency with both sidebands would require a much larger transmitter power output to achieve the same distance.

Note: 10MHz is being used as a simple example for amplitude modulation. 10 MHz is assigned to WWV, the US time standard radio station in Ft Collins, CO, and may not be used for communications by other station.

When we transmit SSB we are eliminating everything but one of the sidebands and then putting all the power capability of the radio into the remaining sideband. This allows us to transmit our message as far as possible. Marine and Ham radios transmit by suppressing the carrier to a minimal level, eliminating one sideband and amplifying only the remaining sideband. So for the example we would transmit only the upper sideband frequency, 10.002MHz for USB or the lower sideband frequency, 9.998MHz for LSB with lots of power.

The remaining sideband is then sent to the output of the radio where it can be amplified to the maximum power of the radio. We put all the power output into the intelligence/modulation of the broadcast. See the next graphic representation below of USB SSB transmitted signal for a single 2 KHz tone.

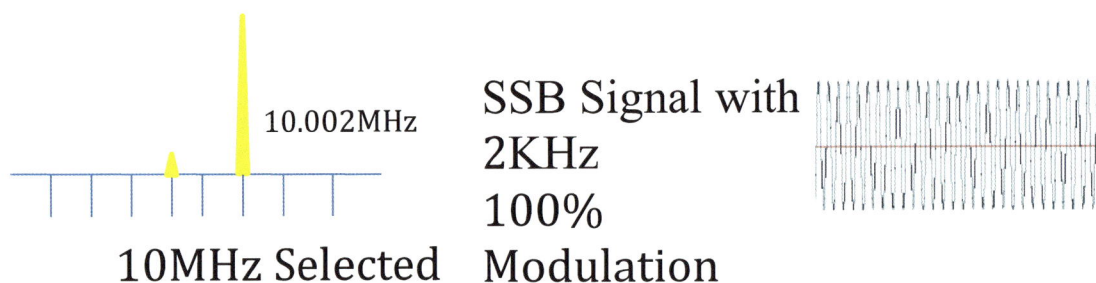

10.002MHz

10MHz Selected

SSB Signal with 2KHz 100% Modulation

When we talk, we put out many frequencies at the same time so the modulation and radio output will change frequency with the voice.

Where Can I Talk
New Hams and Cruisers sometimes think HF SSB radio should be like Marine VHF radio where people are talking on: 13, 16, 9, 68, 69, 71, 72, 78.

Again with over 9,000 possible channels in the HF radio band it is tough to just dial a frequency others are on except for the communications nets which will be discussed later. However, if your favorite AM station is AM 610 (610 KHz), you can probably tune that station in on a typical Marine HF SSB radio.

Another reason new Hams get frustrated and think they cannot hear other stations is that HF radio is long range radio and uses the ionosphere to reflect signals back to the earth. There are many locations where the signal is returning to earth and communications will be good. Likewise there will be many locations where the signal is not on the

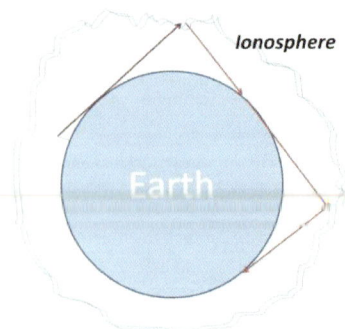

Ionosphere

Earth

earth where you will not be able to hear another station, a dead zone.

The angle at which the radio signal bounces is a function of the frequency transmitted, the Ionosphere layer thickness, the angle of the antenna and type of antenna.

On boats we typically use fiberglass pole antennas or a backstay antenna.   Some shore Ham stations use large beam antennas (they look like big TV antennas) that focus the transmitted and received signals in one direction (where the antenna is pointing).

Side note: In some cases with just the right atmospheric conditions, people hear an echo when they talk on a HF SSB radio.   The echo is because the signal has bounced all the way around the world and came back on the other side as a received signal. Traveling around the world does not happen that often and probably never on a boat, but it is a great example of how the signal can bounce back and forth from the sky to the earth for a long distance.

One test you can do to see if your radio receives stations is to tune the radio into the US time standard, WWV out of Fort Collins, CO. WWV frequencies are broadcast continuously 7X24, 360 days a year on: 2.5MHz, 5MHz, 10MHz, 15MHz, and 20 MHz.   If you are in the Pacific you might also receive WWVH which is transmitted from Hawaii on 25MHz.

Do not plan on getting all the frequencies as they travel via sky waves as explained above.   Only one or two, maybe three, of the frequencies will be present at any particular location.   If you receive one of these stations clearly, your radio reception is probably working OK.

Frequency vs. Meters

A new Ham told me "It is confusing, everything on the Ham test is in meters, but when you start operating your radio, it is all in frequency".

Typical shore based Hams are a bit different than us cruisers. From the test you should know that the meters reference used by Hams is actually referring to a part of a range of frequencies. Shore based Hams buy radio gear and then many of them then focus on putting in antenna systems that cover the area, direction and frequencies they want to talk on. One antenna might be for 120 meters and another for 10 through 20 meters. So meters may be an easier way to think about antenna systems.

While it is easy to understand why Hams use meters instead of frequency references, for a cruiser, it all comes down to being on the right frequency at the right time. For Cruising Hams we have one marginally good HF band antenna that covers all the frequencies we plan to use in MF and HF and one or two VHF antennas for Marine VHF.

Bottom line, cruising Hams have the boat, equipment, and an antenna installed. Our radios are just a tool to communicate with other boats. So we will discuss HF SSB communication primarily in terms of frequency in this book.

Ham Frequencies

In the Marine world, shortcuts to name frequencies have been created for ship to ship stations; e.g. 2A, 2B, 4B, 8A, , , through 25G. The numeric character represents the MHz band and the letter indicating the frequency in that band. In the Ham world, this shortcut is not used. Hams only use frequency and upper/lower sideband to indicate where to transmit and receive.

Appendix III provides the applicable frequency ranges assigned to US Hams based on the different classes of license. The information does not provide cruisers with the information as to what frequency they should select to talk to another boat or shore station. The best frequency to used will be discussed later.

As stated earlier, HF frequencies bounce off the Ionosphere and the earth. If you are hearing a station and move 100 miles closer to the transmitter, you may no longer hear that station as you may now be in a dead zone. You could also move 100 miles the other way and also be in a dead zone.

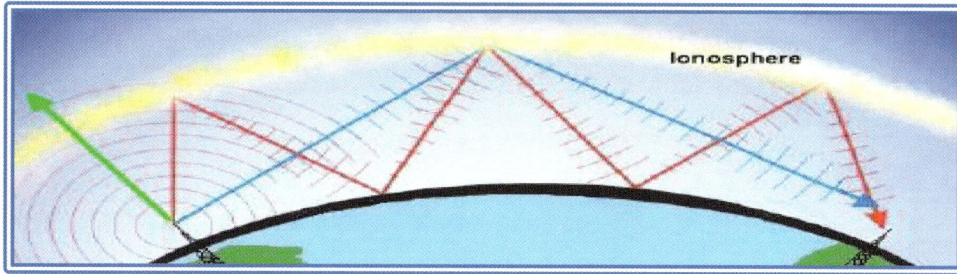

As the Ionosphere changes, you may all of a sudden hear a station clearly that you never heard before.   Some say transmitting and receiving HF radio signals is really a bit of magic.   And most of the time it is magic.

As shown in the picture above HF transmission of the radio signal is propagated in sky waves bouncing off the ionosphere and the earth's surface. The signal also propagates a smaller distance via a ground wave that moves along the surface of the earth. As on the picture, the sky wave will leave dead spots for communications while the signal is bouncing off the Ionosphere.

Below is a table to help you see how frequency and distance play a part in HF radio transmission. However, no table exists that will say this is exactly what you will get, however the table should give you an idea of the way HF signals are effected by frequency and time of day.

MHZ	APPROX RANGE		Ground Wave
	Sky Waves		**Ground Wave**
2 MHz	100 miles day	1000 miles night	150 miles
4 MHz	100 miles day	1500 miles night	100 miles
6 MHz	500 miles day	1500 miles night	75 miles
8 MHz	700 miles day	2000 miles night	70 miles
12 MHz	100 miles evenings	3000 miles days	50 miles
17 MHz	Unreliable evenings	4000 miles days	50 miles
22 MHz	Daytime only band	worldwide	~50 miles

This table is only a rough guide and not a law of propagation. To increase your probability of communications on HF SSB, software tools have been developed that provide calculations based on frequency, time of day, and the distance between two locations.   In spite of the great calculations, you may still not be able to communicate between the two locations because of other variables such as high noise levels, other vessels, hills, etc.

Interference to be Expected

 When sitting in a marina or even at a crowded anchorage, "the Aluminum Forest", you can experience poor transmission and high levels of reflected power, Standing Wave Ratio (SWR) in your radio when transmitting. The masts and stays are excellent reflectors. So if you transmit and get high SWR or maybe just cannot reach anyone from a marina, you may have too many obstacles keeping you from propagating and receiving a good signal.

Another case where you can get high SWR and/or reflected signals is when you are anchored near high cliffs. There is an anchorage in Mexico called Aqua Verde. When at anchor in the southern anchorage there are very big rock cliffs that can make transmission and reception very poor. I always get high SWR on some frequencies in Aqua Verde.

What Frequency do I use

If you have this question, you are not alone. We are all looking for the best frequency to use for communications.

Unfortunately, it is not a simple answer. The variables that come into play are mostly out of our control, except what frequency we plan to use. The main variables to the answer include: The angle of the antenna and the directional characteristics of the antenna (usually set on a boat); time of day; time of year; solar spots and flares, distance to the other station.

To increase the probability of HF communications, there are software applications that you can purchase. The applications calculate the best guess as to what frequencies will work best for the distance between two stations. The distance between stations is typically defined as the difference of Latitude and Longitude between two stations.

For a given distance, propagation programs display a range of frequencies that might work! I am inclined to think that propagation programs really tell you which frequencies will clearly not work.

When you are out at sea, propagation programs may seem to work better as there is not much to block or reflect the signal other than the sky and the water.

In a marina it can be even more difficult to receive than transmit. The incoming signal is very small.   A few things that will impact your HF SSB received signal include: sailboat masts, large boat hulls, metal boats, electrical noise from boats, electrical noise from the marina, nearby hills and mountains, buildings, and in general even the shorelines. These obstacles will affect both the sky wave and the ground wave parts of your transmission.

4.   Cruising with HF SSB

Ham Band Allocations

If you do not have a General class Ham license you should consider obtaining the license in your home country before you go cruising. The General Class License in the United States will allow you to use the 10, 12, 15, 17, 20, 30, 40, 80, and 160 Meter bands. These are bands that are available on marine HF SSB transceivers and where you will find Ham communications nets all over the world.

Modern marine radios cover 1.6 MHz to 29.9 MHz.   The 1.6 MHz to 29.9 MHz will cover the upper part of the Medium Frequency (MF) band and almost all of the High Frequency (HF).

As a cruiser, we only have to dial in the right frequency on our marine radio to communicate. No meter translation is required so after taking the test to get your license, forget about meters. As a result there is very little reference to meters in this book.

Note to Cruisers: *With only a United States issued Technician License, you will not be able to use your HF SSB radio effectively for Ham radio frequencies and Ham communications Nets.*

In some countries the Power and Frequencies may vary with classes of licenses. For example in Mexico they have three classes of Ham license, but all classes may use all Ham frequencies at different levels of maximum output power. E.g. As you advance to the next level, you may transmit with more power.   When you get a reciprocal license in Mexico, a licensed US Technician will be awarded a Mexican Novus reciprocal license. That means you can use your HF SSB in Mexico (only) and join the HF SSB Ham nets. However, twelve miles off shore the US license will apply and you are restricted from using the HF frequencies again.   So be sure and obtain a license that will let you use HF frequencies all the time.

Important Note to Cruisers: The Ham License you earn is good for your home country only.   If you are within the territorial waters of another country you will probably need an additional license to talk on Ham radio frequencies.

In some countries you must apply for a reciprocal license and the license may have a fee you must pay in addition to filing your application.   They give you their countries license based on your countries license level.

Transmitting in another country without a reciprocal license is the same as transmitting in your country without a Ham license. If caught there may be fines and possibly removal of all the communications equipment on your boat.

HF SSB Equipment for Cruisers

This book is not intended to be used for buying and installing Marine radio equipment. However, Hams by default are typically expected to understand HF SSB boat technology at a basic level. As a result this section of the book is intended to provide a basic overview of HF SSB technology used on cruising boats.

Using a Ham Radios

Many old Hams advise cruisers to purchase a Ham radio and not a Marine radio to go cruising. That advice was probably valid twenty years ago as the Marine radios were extremely simple and could not be used for anything except Marine radio frequencies. With only a marine radio a cruiser could miss out on the many Ham nets. For a cruiser starting twenty years ago, a Ham radio would have enhanced the overall safety at sea, but not today.

A recommendation for the average cruiser to purchase "Ham" radio equipment for cruising is poor advice!

Things to consider before you purchase radio equipment for your boat if you are thinking about Ham equipment.

1. Your Ships Station license is a license that allows you to operate type accepted marine equipment.
    a. In order to use a Ham radio it must be illegally modified from its type acceptance to cover marine bands. This is not consistent with the Ships Station license and could be a communications regulatory commission violation.
2. The Ham radios are not pre-programmed with the International Telecommunications Union (ITU) marine channels.
    a. Many of these channels are assigned to stations within the marine infrastructure such as the Coast Guard and marine telephone operators.
    b. It is not possible to program all the ITU channels and the other channels you need for cruising into a Ham radio as the typical Ham radio has no dedicated area for the ITU channels.

3. Ham radios typically have fewer memory locations to store important frequencies. Marine radios tend to have at least 160 locations
4. Ham radios typically output only 100 watts.
    a. Marine radios output 150 watts.
5. Ham radios are usually too complex for the average cruiser. They have more knobs, buttons, and switches than a Marine radio.
    a. Many of the controls have multiple functions making it even more difficult.
    b. The manuals are usually written in *Radio Geek* as it is expected that a Radio Geek will be operating them. As a result I have spent many hours translating cruiser's Ham radio manuals from Radio Geek into cruiser English so that the cruiser can operate and program their radio.
    c. Some of the controls on a Ham radio such as microphone gain can get you into trouble when communicating.
    d. Even if you are a seasoned highly technical Ham, if something happens to you while cruising and communications falls to the less technical person on the boat, a Ham radios can be very challenging for those less technical people.
6. Ham radios do not provide automatic adjustments to assure proper operation like Marine radios.
7. While Ham radios are fully capable of HF SSB email, it can be challenging even for Hams.
8. Marine radios are designed to keep everything as simple as possible.
9. Using a marine radio will allow a new Ham to think about cruising instead of training to be a Radio Geek.
10. Ham radios do not have Digital Selective Calling capability which is a great tool to contact other cruisers and to simplify EMERGENCY/DISTRESS calls in the event of an emergency on your boat.
11. Bottom Line: If you and the other members of your crew plan to spend many hours learning to use a Ham radio, the Ham radio will work on a boat. However, if you want to use your HF SSB radio as a tool to be used on a boat for communications and emergencies get a marine radio with DSC capability.

If you are a long term shore based Ham and plan only to use your HF SSB radio for Ham frequency use only, a Ham radio will work fine on your boat and is legal.   Only having access to Ham frequencies will however result in missing out on the Marine HF SSB nets. You will also have minimal access for help at sea via HF SSB radio.

Using a Marine Radios

Modern marine radios cover all the frequencies and operating modes you need while you are cruising and much more.   Marine radios are "Type Accepted" to cover Ham and Marine band frequencies. No hardware modifications are required to use a Marine radio for the radio to work across the HF band.

Most cruisers use Icom HF SSB marine radios.   The IC M700 Pro, IC M710, and the IC M802 are the majority of radios on cruising boats.

The Icom IC M802 is a powerful radio and can be legally opened up for Ham frequencies with a simple ten second procedure pressing a few buttons on the radio control at the same time. The radio also includes Digital Selective Calling (DSC) which significantly enhances your ability to contact other vessels, get help in an emergency, and learn about safety issues in the area you are travelling.

There are other venders that sell DSC ready HF SSB radios however; the prices I have seen on the internet are significantly higher than the Icom IC M802.   All of the HF SSB DSC capable radios I have found on cruising boats have been Icom IC M802.

The IC M700 Pro and IC M710 are good radios, but are no longer supported by Icom. They can both be found in the used market at a low dollar cost.   The IC M710 is a more flexible radio for cruisers than the IC M700 Pro.   The Icom IC M802 is a giant step in technology over the IC M710.

If you are costal sailing and cash is tight, consider the M710 instead of moving to a Ham radio. If you are heading across an ocean the IC M802 is the radio you should have aboard.

Antenna

There are several different methods used for antennas by Cruisers. Most sailboats use the backstay as the antenna by using insulators to isolate the antenna portion of the backstay from the grounded mast and other rigging.

Vessels with no back stays have used the side stays for the same purpose. A short side stay will work, but usually results in poorer communications. On vessels like Hunter's B&R rigging the after most stays on either side have been used effectively for HF SSB communications.

Recently a new antenna has been made available by a company called Gam Electronics called the "GAM / McKim Split Lead Single Side Band Antenna". The Gam antenna slides up a non-isolated stay. This antenna seems to provide good results for HF SSB communications without cutting your backstay for insulators.

Another popular choice for an antenna is the 24 foot fiberglass antenna. The 24 foot fiberglass antenna is typically used on trawlers and occasionally found on some sailboats.

New installations should be verified operational with an SWR meter before using the system. It is a good idea to also check the antenna system occasionally in the future as corrosion and/or broken lines can also result in potentially damaging high reflected power.

Ground Plane / Counterpoise/ RF Ground
Just as important as the antenna, a good radio frequency ground plane should be installed on your boat. The basic antenna for a boat is actually a combination of the antenna and the ground plane working together. The antenna tuner then inserts electrical changes to the antenna and RF ground such that the resulting antenna system appears to be the proper electrical length for the frequency being transmitted.

Ground planes come in many varieties, but the best ones are those that are totally isolated from the vessel's DC and AC grounds. Some vessels tie all metal items on their boats via copper strapping to each other and then to the ground lug on the tuner. This type of ground can result in poor output and high reflected power on some or all frequencies. It can also increase interference to other electronic equipment on board as this method combines AC, DC, and Radio frequency grounds.

The best grounding system available is a metal boat. They always have good contact with the water and lots of metallic surface area.

While cruising I have found that boats with large copper plating added at the bottom of the boat or mesh put into the hull and not connected to any DC or AC ground seem to be almost as good as a metal boat. Boats in the same area with all types of grounds do not hear as far or transmit as far as the ones with large plates. However, many boats have no place to put the sheets of metal so must revert to other methods.

Most of the other ground systems seem to provide about the same results. They include Dynaplates, radial grounds, copper straps, or strapping to a metal through- hull.

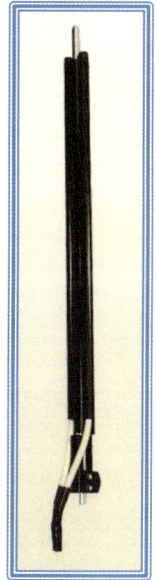

18

Another system used is the stringing of 4" copper foil throughout the boat. This method seems to work for some boats. Some boat manufactures lay the 4" copper along the entire bottom of the boat when the boat is built to make the boat HF SSB ready.

Dynaplates are metal plates that are installed on the bottom of your boat with bolt connections through the hull. To install Dynaplates, the boat must be out of the water. In some cases sailors have used two Dynaplates, one on each side of the boat, to assure water connection while healing. If you install a Dynaplate or two, do not make connections to other parts of the boat.

Some boats have had good luck by connecting a ground strap to a single through- hull with copper straps. In this system, go to one through-hull that will remain under water even when healing. Do not use a bonded through-hull as it will tie you back into the DC ground. Not bonding may result in issues with the valve so this is not my recommended approach.

Radial grounds are wires that are cut to ¼ wave length for each range of frequency. A minimum number for a boat would be wires cut for 2, 4, 6, 8, 10, 12, 14, 16, 18, 20, 22, 24 MHz. When I built mine I also added a wire for each communications net I planned on talking on. A better system would be to double the number so 1, 2, 3, 4, etc. MHz This method works, but is very challenging to put together and install.

All connections on a boat are subject to corrosion. As corrosion builds the radios effectiveness will decrease. All boats are different and I have made measurements on many different boats with all types of grounding systems. When the installation is starting to have issues, it shows up as increased reflected power.

The only ground I have seen that seems to have good reflected power on all the boats I have measured is the KISS-SSB ground by Radioteck. The ground is sealed and on most boats even after a year or more there appears to be no detectable corrosion.

The KISS-SSB ground is not really a ground but radials cut for the different HF bands. It is extremely easy to install and seems to provide good communications.

Because this method does not corrode, even with older installations, the KISS ground tends to have minimal reflected wave. Minimum reflected wave will provide the maximum power to the antenna tuner. The actual system capability is then dependent on the physics of your antenna and ground as they work together to receive and transmit signals.   If using a KISS-SSB ground, do not connect any other ground to the antenna tuner ground lug other than the KISS-SSB connector.

Unfortunately, I have never compared field strengths on different grounds as that would be a major undertaking, but would be the true test. I suspect radial grounds would not measure as well as a metal boat and copper plating, but they do seem to work well based on my cruising experience.

For a non-technical cruiser the Kiss-SSB ground and the Gam backstay antenna may provide the best solution as they are almost maintenance free.

Antenna Tuner
I have found a few boats trying to make do with a manual tuning device they inherited with the purchase of their boat. If you were lucky enough to get a manual tuner with you boat, sell it to a shore based Ham.

Manual Tuner

While it is possible to use a manual tuner, it can make life very difficult to get your radio on the air.   It is also important that the rest of the components can be tuned in for a specific frequency as the manual tuners seem to have a more limited range than the automatic tuners.   I do not recommend manual tuners for cruisers.

Automatic Tuner

The automatic tuners do just that, tune your antenna system properly when transmitting. They are also installed close to the antenna so that maximum power is always transferred from the radio to the antenna, with minimal loss in the coaxial cable.

If you have equipment on board already and do not have an automatic tuner, consider buying one.   Buy a tuner that matches the radio you are using. The tune button on your radio will then allow you to easily pre-tune the system before talking.

DSC Antenna (DERA)

On DSC capable radios such as the Icom IC M802, there is a second receiver built into the radio that scans the emergency digital frequencies for incoming DSC Distress, Urgent, and Ship Safety messages.

This receiver requires a separate antenna to receive the messages. The antenna I call the DSC Emergency Reception Antenna (DERA) must be attached to hear emergency signals.

Note to Cruisers: All other DSC reception and transmission is completed by the normal transmitting antenna. (Stay mounted antenna or 24 foot whip.) So you can use all of the DSC functions on your radio with your normal antenna. You will not be able to hear emergency calls or responses to your emergency calls without a DERA.

If you have an Icom IC M802 and no DERA, check out my website on the Icom page for a procedure to make a home-made unit. It is better than nothing.

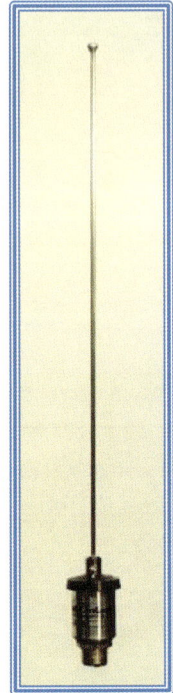

GPS Connection

If you have a DSC equipped radio, you need to make sure your GPS signal is connected to HF SSB radio as well as your VHF radio. No one will respond to an emergency call if you do not provide the position information with the emergency call.

Programming HF SSB Radio for Ease of Use

Depending on where you are planning to cruise, the radios may include most of what you need, but it may not be in any real order. As a result a notebook must be maintained so you know where the channels are. Too hard for me!

It will make your life much easier if you pre-program your HF SSB radio with the channels you need for your planned cruising area. This includes the frequencies that the international Search and Rescue (SAR) groups monitor for emergencies. Having the SAR frequencies pre-programmed will allow you to hail for help in an emergency and then shift to the appropriate working channel as defined by the responding station by just rotating your channel knob.

You should also pre-program the Communication Nets; Time standard; and marine operator(s) for the area you plan to visit. Most Marine radios come programmed with all the user channels full, but most of these frequencies are of little value to a typical cruiser.

Most radios come pre-programmed with some good things, but many other frequencies such as Great Lakes traffic and the Mississippi River control do not do much for the average cruiser.

My recommendation is to delete all the programmed channels and start over with something that makes sense based on where you are heading. This process is much simpler if you purchase the programming software and interface cable for your radio.

Recommended Programming

The key is to lose that sheet of paper, so I developed a basic programming scheme so it was Made Simple for Cruisers. Where ever you are if you use this format it will be simple to find what you need without a separate book. Be sure and program the labels that will make sense to you later. This will eliminate the need for a user channel record sheet.

HF SSB Programming – Made Simple for Cruisers

1-20 Safety at Sea related Coast Guard Calling Frequencies then Working Frequencies followed by the country you are going to Coast Guard or Navy Calling and Working frequencies.

- Types of labels to consider CG4, CG 8, CG WK 4, to indicate Coast Guard or Coast Guard Working on 4 MHz, 8MHz, etc.

The calling frequencies are "Simplex Channels". (Transmit and receive frequency are the same.) Working Channels are "Duplex Channels". (Transmit and receive frequency are different.) Duplex channels are typically channels that are used to talk ship to a shore station. Many shore stations have separate transmitters and receivers so they can hear everything you are saying, even if they are trying to talk over you.

21-80 I reserved for Ship to Ship, as I call them, ABC channels. E.g. 2A, 2B, 2C,. . . . . , 25F, 25G. (The number represents frequency band in MHz and the letter identifies a specific frequency within the band.) See table in Appendix XIII for all the frequencies.

- Labels to consider, use the actual Name: 2A, 2B, ...25G

Programming these channels sequentially will allow you to go directly to the channel when someone says I will meet you on 6A.

80-100 I have left mostly empty to allow an area for other favorite frequencies that may be added later. However, at the end of this group I program 2.5MHz, 5MHz, 10MHz, 15MHz, 20MHz, and 25MHZ which is the US time standard, WWV and WWVH. The time standard stations are located here as the next group is where the HF SSB

Communications Nets start. This will allow the operator to quickly check the time before tuning in a communications net.

101-120 are set aside for HF SSB Nets, both marine and Ham nets. Channel 101 is programmed with the first net in the morning, 102 is the next one of the day and so on. Put in a blank channel occasionally to allow you to set up a special frequency for a net without modifying your base programming.

- Label recommendations: Use the name of the net plus for alternate frequencies of a net use a portion of the frequency that will differentiate the channel e.g. Amigo is on 8122 with a backup frequency of 8A and 8B. Amigo Net also uses what they refer to as a short range frequency of 4B so the label for those channels might be Amigo22, Amigo8A, Amigo8B, and Amigo4B respectively.

121+ I program the Marine HF SSB operators so I can make a phone call if I need to. In the US we use WLO radio and KLB radio. While they all have assigned ITU channels, To keep it simple without paper, programing all the marine operators channels into your radio.

- Labeling recommendations: WLO plus the ITU channel number e.g. WLO1212.

On my web site you will find an example of the user channel assignments that follow my Made Simple for Cruisers approach. The example is for the Pacific Coast Cruisers heading for the United States and Sea of Cortez Mexico Cruiser.

Voice Communication with HF SSB

It would be great if I could say just go to channel 16 and everyone will be there.   Unfortunately, HF SSB is not that easy. You cannot just go to a channel or frequency and start calling a friend or wait for someone else to come on like Marine VHF.   There is also no place to go and get a radio check like on Marine VHF.

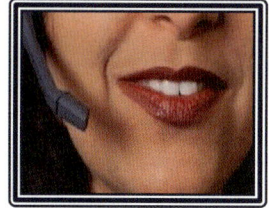

HF SSB Communications Nets, email, phone calls, weather information, wind information, and position reporting are probably the main uses of HF SSB for cruisers. With a Ham radio license, all of these tasks may be completed at no additional cost. We will discuss how to get started for each of these uses in the sections that follow.

This section will discuss how to communicate via voice and identify some tools for improving the probability of talking.

5. Making Voice Calls

"How do I contact another boat on HF?   Again, there is no frequency that everyone congregates on for HF SSB.   As a result many new Hams and even non Hams using Marine bands can get very frustrated with HF SSB radio. I keep hearing "There is no one on the radio".   Remember there are many potential frequencies to use on HF SSB. Even though there are many Hams and Marine band users, you may never find one if you just start tuning the radio all over the HF band.   You may hear fax machines, music, multiplex signals, people talking in foreign languages, and maybe even some people talking in your countries language, but not necessarily another cruiser looking to talk to you.

Voice Calling Options

Some cruisers start flipping through the channel knob which displays the pre-programmed frequencies by Icom.   You could sit on many of those channels and never hear anyone for months.   That is why the earlier section on pre-programming your radio was provided. Your radio needs to have frequencies programmed that are relevant to where you are cruising.

Since HF radio covers so many possible frequencies you can talk on, cruisers have found three ways to be able to talk to friends and get information.   These methods are hailing during or after a communications net, establishing a time and frequency to call (Make a Date), and the new more effective approach is Digital Selective Calling.

To hail a friend on a net you first have to be able to legally get onto the net. There are Marine radio nets and Ham nets so make sure you are on a net consistent with the license(s) you have and you are using the appropriate call sign for the net. Marine band call signs have letters then numbers and Ham call signs have letters, a number and more letters.

Rules to Follow

Actually there are not a lot of rules to follow when using your HF SSB while cruising. The rules are those you learned to pass the Ham test and the rest are just common communications courtesy.

1. **Use your call sign.** This is a basic requirement of being a Ham. You must use your call sign. When talking on VHF and even some times Marine HF SSB, the call signs may not be used, but they are in fact supposed to be used for all radio communications. Other Hams will typically not talk to you if you do not use your call sign, except in an emergency.

2. **Be courteous on the radio**. Listen before you talk. If someone else is using the channel, wait.

3. If you need to **add to an ongoing conversation**, wait for a lull and call out "Break, Break". Only if acknowledged by a member of the ongoing conversation, you may proceed.

4. When participating in a communications net, the **net control station** coordinates all other stations transmitting.

5. If someone asks for a **signal report**, be honest and do not just try and make them feel good.

6. When finished talking, remember to **sign off with your call sign**. Something like: "This is AD7XL and I am clear."

See Appendix XVI for a basic procedure to get started transmitting.

Typical Signal Level Reports

Readability Scale		Signal Strength Scale	
1	Hardly perceptible; unreadable	1	Unintelligible; barely perceptible
2	Weak; readable now and then	2	Weak signals; barely readable
3	Fairly good; readable but with difficulty	3	Weak signals; but can be copied
4	Good; readable	4	Fair signals
5	Very good; perfectly readable	5	Fairly good signals
		6	Good signals
		7	Moderately strong signals
		8	Strong signals
		9	Extremely strong signals

Joining HF SSB Communications Nets

Communications Nets

Most cruisers participate in Communications Nets on VHF and HF SSB. The VHF nets typically occur in marinas and major cruiser locations and are port specific.

HF SSB Communications Nets occur all over the world at different times and frequencies. The missions of all the nets are usually similar, but may very slightly in protocol. Higher frequency Communications Nets, greater than 7 MHz, are typically longer range nets, out into the Pacific or Atlantic. The lower frequency Communications Nets, less than 7 MHz, are generally more of a region or area net like the Sea of Cortez, Caribbean, BaHamas, Hawaiian Islands etc.

The Communications Nets provide a means for cruisers to find out what is going on in the area they are cruising. For example: what is the weather going to do; availability of anchorages; local things happening; etc.

The Communications Nets also provide a time and frequency where cruisers may make contact with other cruisers.   If both cruisers can hear the net, they can probably exchange information between each other during or after the net.

When the sun is coming up during early morning nets the communication ranges can change. This is because the sun heats the ionosphere and the F1 and F2 layers start separating resulting in a change in the reflected signal.   Sometimes it may be better to get a quick message to a friend during or before an early morning net rather than after the net when the ionosphere changes and you can no longer reach your friend. However, depending on the distance between your two boats, it may actually be better communications after the net is over.

Note to Cruisers: Most Nets are controlled Nets. That means you must ask Net Control for permission to talk and/or call a friend.

I have posted on www.Made-simplefor-Cruisers.com a net schedule in Excel format that you may download and modify to meet your cruising needs. It can be found on the upper right hand corner of the "Communications" tab.

Zulu	Local Time Difference**	Name	Frequency USB/LSB Alternate Freqency	Coverage	Comments	WEB Site
Winter / Summer	5:00					Updated 12SEP2012
~ 24 X7		14.300 Nets	14.300 USB	East/West/South	Interncontinental / Maritime Mobile / Pacific Seafarers	http://14300.net
11:00 / 12:00	6:00 / 7:00	Intercon	14.300 USB	Carib & Pacific	From 07:00 - 12:00 ET	http://interconnet.org/
13:30	8:30	Picante	6.212 USB	Mexico	Net controls Puerto Vallarta.	N/A
14:00	9:00	Pan Pacific	8.143 USB 8.137 USB 8.155 USB	Central America	Pacific: South Pacific to Panama, Ecuador & the Galapagos and occasionally out to South Pacific.	N/A
14:00	9:00	Amigo	8.122 USB 8.294 USB 8.297 USB	Mexico	Mexico and Puddle Jumpers (Alt Frequencies 8A and 8B)	N/A
14:30	9:30	Amigo	4.149 USB	Mexico	Approximate Time for Short-range net	N/A
14:30 / 13:30	9:30 / 8:30	Sonrisa	3.968 LSB	Mexico	Weather at UTC 13:45 Summer & 14:45 Winter.	http://sonrisanet.org/
15:30	10:30	Chubasco	7.192 LSB	Mexico	Warmup.	N/A
15:00 / 16:00	10:00 / 11:00	Baja California	7.2335 LSB	Mexico	Weather 15:15 / 16:15.	N/A
16:00	11:00	USCG Amature	14.300 USB		Saturday Only	http://www.w5cgc.org/
17:00 / 16:00	12:00 / 11:00	Maritime Mobile Service	14.300 USB	Carib & Pacific	From 17:00 - 03:0, Rene (K4EDX)	http://www.mmsn.org/
17:00	12:00	USCG Amature	14.327 USB		Saturday Only	http://www.w5cgc.org/
18:00	13:00	Manana	14.340 USB	Mexico	Monday-Saturday	http://reocities.com/TheTropics/3989/
21:00	16:00	Pacific Maritime	21.402 USB	Pacific		http://pmmsn.net/
0:00	19:00	Happy Hour	3.968 LSB	Mexico		N/A
0:55	19:55	Southbound	8.122 USB	Mexico	Coverage area: Mexico	http://groups.yahoo.com/group/southbound group
3:00	22:00	Pacific Seafarers	14.300 USB	South Pacific	Warmup 03:00 and roll-call 3:25 for underway vessels	http://www.pacseanet.com/
						Made Simple for Cruisers

** Enter offset from UTC as a positive value, e.g. -7 hours is entered as "7:00".

	Marine SSB		www.made-simplefor-cruisers.com
Summer	Amature SSB	Winter	

West Coast Schedule 2-22-2013 (in Net Start Time of Day Order)

Within the spreadsheet, there are also links to home pages for the nets, when available. The web pages can provide additional information for the area covered by the net. The net schedule covers West Coast, South Pacific, East Coast, Bahamas to Panama and Panama Communications Net schedules.

Note to Cruisers: *If you find a change or correction needed, please let me know so we can all help each other cruise better.*

p-t_on_sunyside@live.com

Ham Band Nets

Ham radio Communications Nets require a Ham license to transmit. However, even if you do not have a Ham license you can always listen and gain valuable information.

The Ham Communications Nets also provide weather and other information needed by cruisers. There are more Ham Communications Nets than Marine nets in most areas.

Taking part in both Ham and Marine band nets will provide you with the best chance of getting the cruising information you may need.

In an Emergency you may transmit on any Frequency to get help, without a license.

In an EMERGENCY you may use any means possible to communicate your needs for help. So even if you do not have a Ham license now, program the Ham Net channels into your radio for the area you are or plan to cruise within.

Some examples of Ham HF SSB Communications Nets for the west coast and Pacific side of Mexico:

Name	Time UTC	Frequency	Mode
Sonrisa	13:30	3968.0KHz	LSB*
Chubasco	15:00	7192.0KHz	LSB*
Pacific Maritime	22:00	21402.0KHz	USB*
Maritime	Hourly	14300.0KHz	USB*

* Ham Radio uses Lower Sideband (LSB) on lower Frequencies and USB on higher channel frequencies.

The 14,300 KHz Net starts at 7:00 AM ET with Intercon net then switches to the Maritime net after a few hours. The net continues all day and in the evening it changes to the Pacific Seafarers Net which lasts until about 10:00 PM ET. Even if they are not officially on the air, there is probably someone from the net listening on 14,300 KHz if you need help.

As a Ham, 14,300 KHz Hams will do phone patches and relays to help you out, as long as your request is not commercially related. If you ask, the Net Controller will also post your position on Yotreps so your family knows where you are located.

Communications Net Protocol
New Hams have told me that they are concerned about making a mistake when they call other folks on the radio or check into a net.

Here are some tips to allow you to get started talking on the nets. Don't be afraid of making a mistake, it is only other cruisers listening. If you never check in you are missing a great opportunity to make some new friends.

Things to Get Ready to talk on a Net
1. Go to a couple of Ham nets and listen to the protocol. Usually the protocol is similar.

     a. In some cases the net control person wants you to call out your call-sign suffix (The letters after the number in your call sign).

     b. On other nets, you will be requested to call out your entire call sign.

2. The net control person is the person that controls who talks on the net and when.

     a. At some time they will say something like "I am taking check ins now" or maybe "check ins from Texas may check in now".

     b. Location check ins may be used for large nets to reduce the number of stations talking over each other, "Pile-Ups" (Pile-Ups =More than one station is trying to transmit at the same time.)

3. Most nets have a mission so pay attention to the mission.

     a. Here in Mexico, most cruisers share weather information for their location to aid other cruisers potentially moving to that area.

     b. Longer range nets may be focused on, for example cruisers headed to the South Pacific. The Net will get position and weather information to and provide to other "Puddle Jumpers".

4. Using the Communications Net as a place to meet, you can keep in touch with your friends on other boats.

5. Make sure you know the phonetic alphabet for your call sign, your vessel name, and the names of the people on board. See Appendix IV. Do not make up your own words as they can be confusing. E.g. Terry is Tango; Echo; Romeo; Romeo; Yankee. Other cruisers can recognize these standard words where Tides; Everyone; Really; Really, Yahoo would probably be confusing and require a repeat transmission for clarity.

Example of Protocol within a Communications Net

I will be using my boat, s/v Sunnyside and my call sign AD7XL for this example.

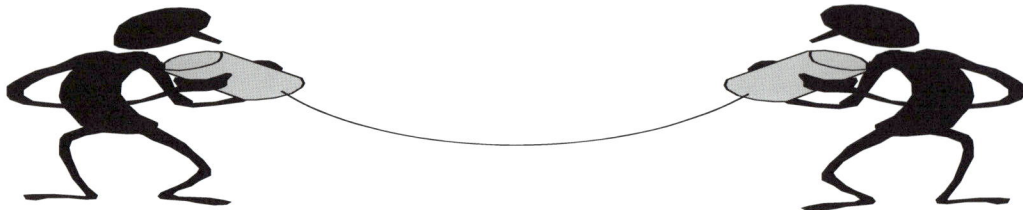

- **Net Control:** Vessels may check in now.

- **Sunnyside:** X-ray Lima (or for some nets the whole call sign e.g. Alpha Delta seven X-ray Lima.)
- **Net Control:** X-ray Lima, please check in now.
- **Sunnyside:** This is Alpha Delta seven X-ray Lima, Terry and Patricia on the sailing vessel Sunnyside presently located in Puerto Vallarta. The temperature here is 85 degrees in the cabin, 60% humidity, and the barometer (bar) is at 1016. The wind last night was out of the northwest at about ten knots and this morning it has fallen off to peeks of five knots from the northwest. The pool (water temp) is 78 degrees.
    a. If at an anchorage the clarity of the water may be added.
- **Net Control:** What is the sky doing?
- **Sunnyside:** We have very few fluffy clouds right now, but it was mostly overcast last night.
- **Net Control:** Do you have any traffic?
- **Sunnyside:** Yes, I would like to call Motor Vessel Gracias.
- **Net Control:** Ok make your call.
- **Sunnyside:** Kilo Tango six Whiskey Whiskey Yankee, this is Alpha Delta seven X-ray Lima.
- **Sunnyside and Gracias:** (plain talk discussion after Gracias answers and calls out their call sign)
- **Gracias:** This is Kilo Tango six Whiskey Whiskey Yankee clear and we will be on the side.

- **Sunnyside:** when complete with traffic:

31

This is Alpha Delta seven X-ray Lima Clear and we will be on the side.

➢ **Net Control:** Thank you for clearing, any other check-ins call back with your suffix now.

For a new Ham this may seem a bit structured, but it is easy to get into the swing of things. With a little practice and use of the phonetic alphabet it eliminates having to say things over and over to be understood.

The worst thing that can happen is you might say "a,a,a," or say a word wrong, but no one really cares as <u>we are all cruisers</u>. The other cruisers will appreciate your checking in and helping with the weather picture for the area and anchorage information.

After you have received permission from Net Control to talk or made contact with another vessel and both stations have announced their call signs; feel free to just use plain talk and forget the protocol until you are ready to clear the frequency. However if you are transmitting information to the other party, the phonetic alphabet will help your communications and minimize the number of requests for you to repeat your last information.

When you are ready to end the call, announce your call sign and say clear.

This is Alpha, Delta, 7, X-ray, Lima, Clear!

Make a Date Call with Other Cruisers

Because there are so many possible places to communicate on HF SSB radio, many cruisers establish a time to meet a friend on a specific frequency. This can still result in trial and error to find the right frequency for the distance you and the other vessel are apart during the specified time of day.

An approach that cruisers often use is what I call "Make a Date". Make a Date is accomplished by emails between parties prior to the time where they agree to meet on a specific frequency at a specified time.

A special kind of Make a Date is where cruisers agree to be on a frequency for a Communications Net as noted above to talk before, during or after the net on the same frequency. If both vessels can hear each other checking into the net, they can probably establish communications together during or after the net.

A trick I have been using is to use the propagation tool in Airmail. Airmail propagation tool can calculate the optimal frequencies to use for voice communication based on the time of day. There is a procedure later in this book to help you to set up the Airmail propagation tool for voice communications.

Propagation tools do not always work perfectly, but they can be a starting tool to help with a "Make a Date" communications call. The real challenge comes when both parties are in an electrically noisy marina. Marinas are notorious for having lots of electrical noise and sailboat masts that bounce the signals around. Unfortunately, marinas are usually where we have internet available allowing us to "Make a Date".

When vessels are traveling together in Open Ocean, but out of marine VHF range, it can be easier to "Make a Date" call. Frequently cruisers set a specified time each day on a specific frequency where they will get together and share information. Having someone else to talk to while on a long transit can make your trip a lot more pleasant.

One example is the Puddle Jumpers net used by boats headed to the South Pacific from the Baja and Puerto Vallarta Mexico. The "Make a Date" method works great for them, but it may actually be more like a special Communications Net.

Getting Phone Patches from Other Hams

As a new Ham you may not be aware of the fact that many shore based Hams also have phone patch equipment.   That means they can and most of the time love the opportunity to help a cruiser make a call.

A good source for Hams with phone patch equipment is to check into a net where you know there are many shore based Hams participating.   The 14,300 KHz Net is active approximately fifteen hours a day seven days a week and provide a good place to try to get a phone patch.   The majority of the Hams on this net are shore based.

A True Sea Story: While two friends, my wife, and I were coming down the Baja California Coast a number of years ago, my wife broke her ankle in Bahia Tortugas (Turtle Bay). My wife and her friend Petra set out in an ambulance to head to La Paz, BCS Mexico.   That is a long story by itself.

While my wife and Petra were traveling to La Paz, Petra's husband, Bob, and I were driving the boat as fast as we could go from Turtle Bay to La Paz.

By checking into the Maritime net on 14.3 MHz every few hours, we were able to make a free phone call to the cell phone that Petra had with her in the ambulance. The phone patch was provided at no cost from a fellow Ham.

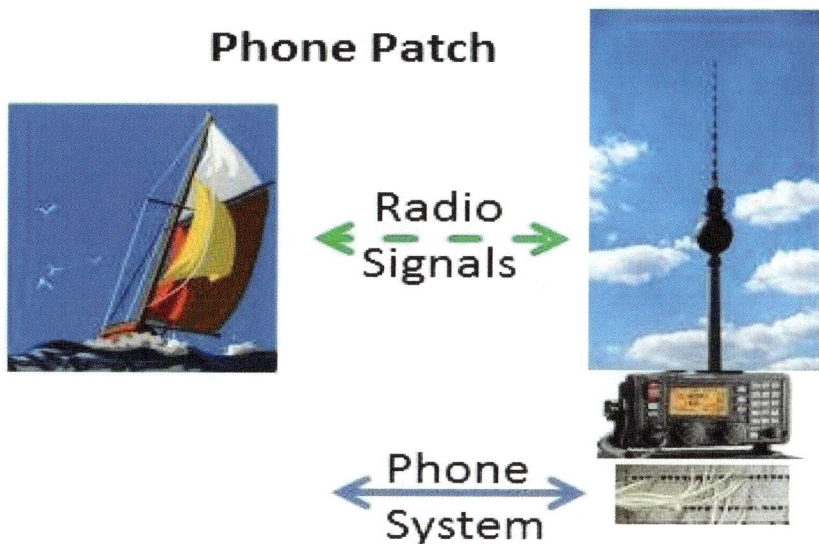

In one case, no one on the net had phone patch equipment. However, one station volunteered to do a phone relay for us. (We ask questions, he asks them on the phone

and relays the answer to us.) It gave Bob and me a lot of peace of mind to learn the status of our ambulance traveling wives.

Don't forget, Hams are a great group and always willing to help in any way they can. Phone patches, relayed messages via HF SSB, relays via phone calls, etc. are just a few things that Hams love to do to help cruisers have a good day at sea.

Propagation Tool to Determine the Best Frequency

Most cruisers are on a tight budget and would like to not spend money on more software as well as have to learn to use a new piece of software. However, if you are using HF SSB radio you need a propagation tool to provide a scientific guess as to what frequencies may be and cannot be used.

If you are using Sailmail and/or Winlink (both products to be discussed later) you may already be using the propagation tool that is provided for the Airmail interface. The propagation tool is used to determine which station/frequency to use for replicating your email.

Note: If you are not using Winlink and or Sailmail, you may have to download the Airmail software from Sailmail before getting started.
Refer to the email section in this book and/or use the steps provided by Sailmail to get the Airmail program working. The download must include the Icepac propagation software in order to utilize the propagation tool.

Airmail uses another free product called Icepac as the calculation engine for the propagation calculations. Icepack needs the latitude and longitude at the two points and sunspot data as input to calculate the reliability percentage and Signal to Noise Ratio (SRN) for every frequency sent from the Airmail propagation tool.

To use the Airmail Propagation tool as a voice communications tool, we need to create two fake email stations within a new group in Airmail. The fake stations we will call Ham Band and Marine Band B.

Within the fake stations you will need to input a list of the frequencies across the HF radio band. The frequencies input will be used by the propagation tool to calculate the propagation picture.

You could just create one table with 2000.0 KH, 4000.0, 6000.0, etc., to 30000.0 and have a rough idea for propagation.

However, to optimize the calculations around the frequencies we plan to use we will use selected frequencies within the Marine and Ham bands that are authorized for voice communications.

Procedure to Make a Propagation Tool

To use the Airmail Propagation tool as a voice communications tool, we will create two fake stations in Airmail called "Ham Band" and "Marine Band B" in a new group we will call "Voice".

The Marine band fake station will use the Ship to Ship "B" channels for each MHz. See table below.

Marine Band

Marine MHz B Channel	Frequency in KHz
2B	2079.0
4B	4149.0
6B	6227.0
8B	8297.0
12B	12356.0
16B	16531.0
18B	18828.0
22B	22162.0
25B	25103.0

For the new fake Ham station we will use the middle of the frequencies within each band plan assignment, for voice communications. See table below.

Ham Bands

Meters	Frequency Range	Center
160 Meters	1.800 - 2.000 MHz	1900.0
80 Meters	3.600 - 4.000 MHz	3800.0
40 Meters	7.125 - 7.300 MHz	7212.5
20 Meters	14.150 - 14.350 MHz	14250.0
17 Meters	18.110 - 18.168 MHz	18139.0
15 Meters	21.200 - 21.450 MHz	21325.0
12 Meters	24.930 - 24.990 MHz	24960.0
10 Meters	28.300 - 29.700 MHz	29000.0

Procedure for Marine Band

1. Start the Airmail Program.
2. With the mouse, click on "**View**"
3. Then click on "**Station List**"
4. Now click "**New**".
5. Type in the field provided <u>Voice</u>.
6. Click "**OK**".
7. Click on "Settings".
8. Type <u>your Call Sign</u> into the field "**Our Callsign**".
9. Click on "**OK**".

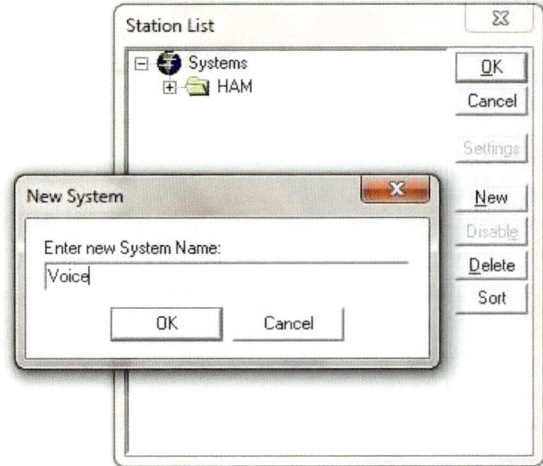

10. Click on "**Voice**"
11. Click on "**New**"

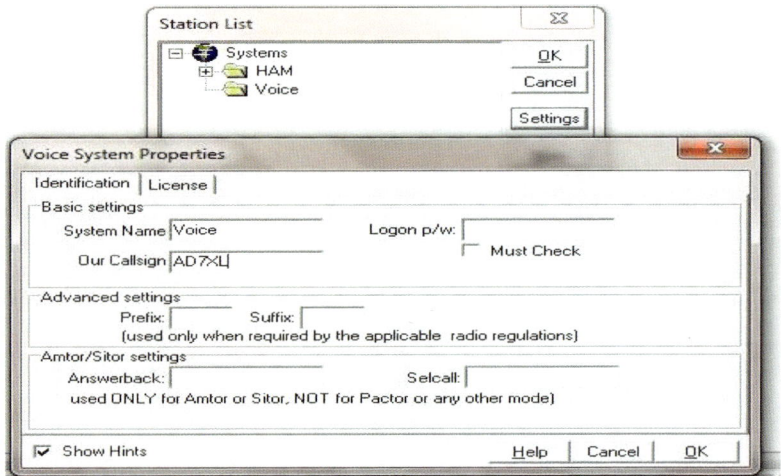

12. Type in <u>Marine Band B</u>
13. Click on "**OK**"
14. Locate the new Station "**Marine Band B**" and click on it to highlight "**Marine Band B**".

15. Click on "Settings".

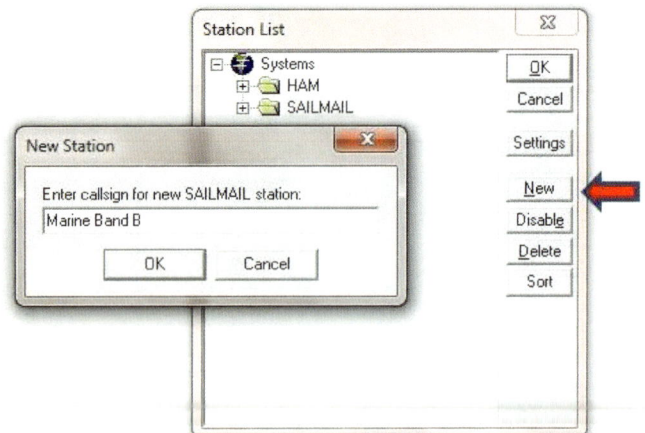

16. Enter the Marine Band frequencies as noted in the table above into the window "Frequencies". E.g. 2079.0, 4149.0, 6227.0, 8297.0, 12356.0, 16531.0, 18828.0, 22162.0, 25103.0

17. Eliminate all the modems and formats, except for clicking on the "**Pactor 3**" checkpoint.
18. Type in the "**Name**" field the text <u>Marine Band B</u> to remind you that these are Ship to Ship "B" channels.
19. The software also requires that the station have a Latitude and Longitude so that the propagation program will include the station in the initial station list.   See note below for suggestions. (This location is not critical as it will be changed when using the program.   Pick some round numbers like: 50° 00' North and 100° 00' West as place holders.)

20. Click "**OK**" to close the window.
21. Click "**OK**" to close the window.

22. Repeat the procedure to implement a Ham Band station and frequencies using the label "Ham Band" in place of "Marine Band B" and the center frequencies from the "Ham" table frequencies above.

You can also add other real stations to analyze propagation spectrums for such as Weather Fax Stations, Marine Operators, etc. The only difference in the process would be that the real stations have actual location that need to be entered into the "Location" window.

Using the Propagation Tool

Now that you have the two fake stations loaded, you can use the Airmail propagation tool to find the best frequencies to use.

1. Start the Airmail program
2. Press the function key "**F8**" (or click on "**View**" and then "**Propagation**")
3. Click on the "+" sign on "**Voice**" to open, if not already open.
4. Find the "**Ham Band**" or "**Marine Band B**" station and click on it.
5. Make sure your latitude and longitude are correct under "**From our location**".
6. Insert the latitude and longitude of the station you are planning to call under the "**To station location**".

Note: The "To station location" latitude and longitude may be slightly different than what we entered when setting up the station. Inside the propagation program it uses a grid system instead of the actual latitude and longitude. So the program modifies the position to the closest grid value and stores that latitude and longitude.

7. Locate the frequencies with the highest "**Reliability**" number (numbered from 0 to the maximum of 100) for communications during the UTC time period you plan to communicate.

Notes:
➤ *The potentially usable frequencies will be colored green and the non-usable frequencies are colored red.*
➤ *Make sure the Sun Spots index is reasonable for the present period.*
➤ *Sunspot Index: http://www.arrl.org/w1aw-bulletins-archive-propagation*

> ➢ *Sunspots are approximately 65-70 In January 2013.*
> ➢ *The time is based on your computer's time, but is in UTC.*
> ➢ *The present time of day is noted on the Propagation chart with a blue highlight on the hour. See arrow below marked "**Time**".*
> ➢ *This program uses a scale of 0 to 100% for reliability of communications between the two locations.*

8. Now click on the "**SNR**" checkmark to change the propagation presentation to the Signal to Noise Ratio (SNR) view. See arrow below marked "**SNR**". To expect reasonable communications, SNR numbers should be greater than 50.

9. Locate the frequencies again that had the highest reliability number and identify which of the frequencies have the highest SNR. Those will be the frequencies with the highest probability for communications.

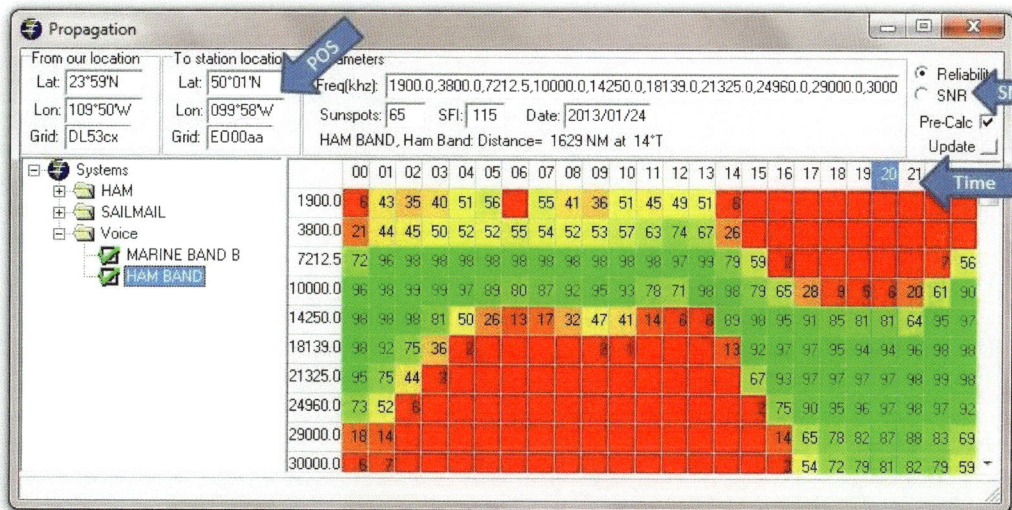

40

Example of Propagation Calculations La Cruz Mexico to La Paz

The following example uses the Ham fake station. For this example we will use a location near La Cruz, Mexico of 20° 43' north and 105° 24' west, for our "**From our location**", and near La Paz, Mexico, for our "**To station location**", of 24° 16' North and 105° 24' West.

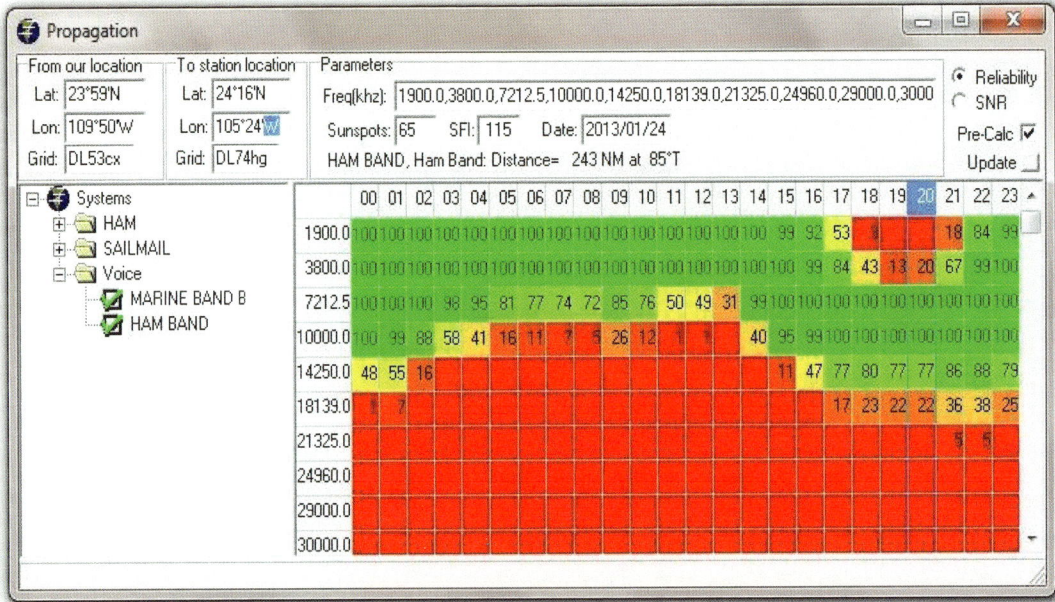

Reliability shows 100% for both 7.2 MHz and 10 MHz for the present 2000 UTS hour.

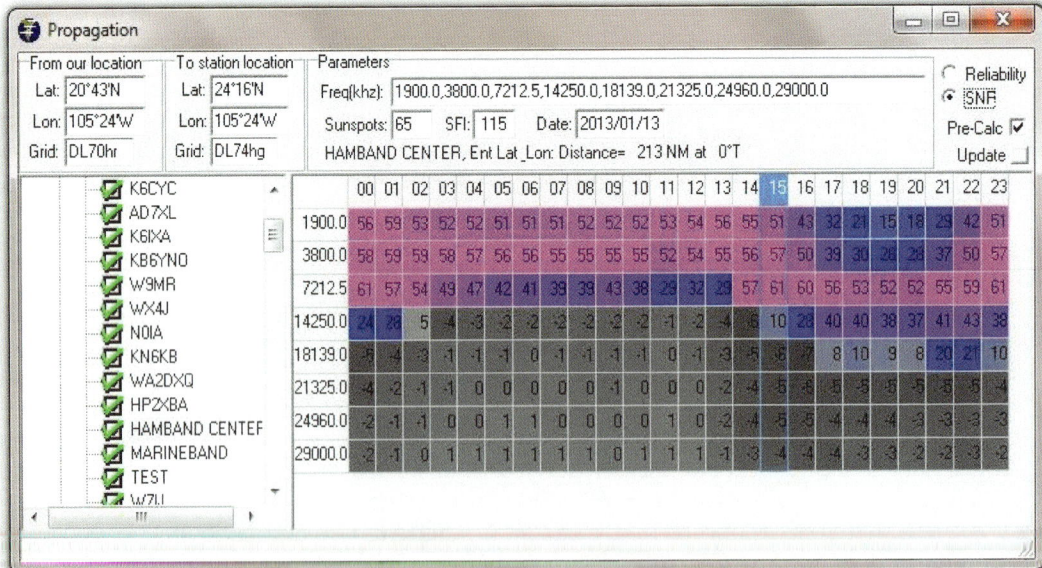

Note: Looking at these graphs, it is clear why the Sonrisa net is on 3968.0 KHz in the morning. That frequency works well for Sonrisa for coverage from Puerto Vallarta to La Paz and La Paz to the north end of the Sea of Cortez

The SNR shows the 7.2 MHz may be better than the 10 MHz at the present time. As a result you may have a higher probability of communications within the 7 MHz band. If that does not work, try something in the 10 MHz band.

There is a good reason why they call HF communications Magic.

Quick Reference for Propagation Checks

Things to do to Find the Best Voice Frequency
- Open Airmail and Press "**F8**"
- Select Voice
- Select Ham or Marine Band B
- Make sure your position is entered correctly.
- Enter the vessel's position/location you are planning to contact.
- When available, check the "**Sunspots**" number. While the sunspot number does not change rapidly it does change over time. (In February 2013 the sunspot number was increasing and approximately ~57)
- Inspect the reliability chart and select frequencies with the highest reliability numbers for the desired time.
- Select the SNR display
- Locate the frequencies with the highest reliability on the SNR chart. By inspection of the highest reliability frequencies select the frequency(ies) with the highest SNR for the desired time.

Start your communication with the frequency with the highest reliability and SNR first. In some cases you may have more than one frequency that have the same numbers, so try them first. If the highest number pair frequency does not work, try the next highest reliability/SNR combination frequency. Hopefully one of the frequencies selected will work. If you are unable to establish communications, you can retry selected frequencies at a different time of the day.

Digital Communications with HF SSB

Digital Communications on HF SSB radio is very common. Cruisers can send and receive emails, get weather faxes, and even text between boats.

This section will discuss these processes and include some basic procedures to get you started with HF SSB Digital.

6. email - Winlink

Basics

Staying in touch with family back home or doing business via email is something many cruisers do daily.   Ham email is free via a Ham supported email system called Winlink 2000.   Winlink is a free service only because it is provided by other Hams who volunteer to buy the equipment and keep it running at no cost to us.

Some Hams also obtain a subscription to Sailmail so they have access to both HF SSB email systems.   Sailmail is a very good service provided at a reasonable annual fee. Sailmail is also the only service available in some areas of the world.

The Both Winlink and Sailmail have HF SSB radios connected to computers all over the world. When you call an email site, the computer and modem controls the remote site and your computer and modem control your site. The two computers send messages back and forth to make sure they understand each other. When they are communicating with each other, your computer will send all of your mail to the Winlink/Sailmail server via the radios.   Upon completion of sending the Winlink/Sailmail server will send you all the information it collected from the internet and forward the mail you sent to the internet for delivery.

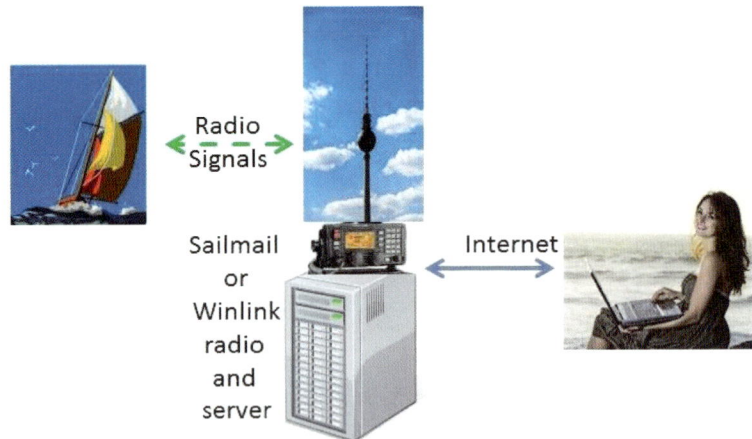

Winlink and Sailmail are basically the same Winlink is based on your Ham License call sign and uses Ham servers. Sailmail is based on the call sign assigned by your Ships Station License and use a different set of servers. The features and functions for both Sailmail and Winlink systems are very similar.   Another difference is that Sailmail servers are connected via Marine assigned frequencies and Winlink servers are connected via Ham assigned frequencies.

Note to Cruisers: Free email is another great reason why getting your General Class License was a good idea.

Both Sailmail and Winlink can use the same user interface software called Airmail. Airmail was written by Jim Corenman and is provided free by Sailmail.   It is a good product and easy for cruisers to learn to use.   Jim Corenman did a great job for us all so many thanks Jim.

There is new software called RMS Express that may be used as an interface to Winlink. The software is very high quality, but in my opinion developed for shore locations. Airmail includes weather fax, dumb terminals and you can modify your position within the propagation tool.   To keep it simple, it is recommended that cruisers use the Airmail software and tools.

If you would like to use both Sailmail and Winlink, the process is very simple.   To use both Winlink and Sailmail download one version of the software set it up and then download the other version and set it up.   The second download will integrate into the first software version and provide the option of receiving and sending email from either Winlink or Sailmail at your discretion. Using both systems will provide a cruiser with more servers around the world.

Airmail also provides a Weather Fax tool, Position reporting tool, Propagation tool, dumb terminal tool, access to weather tool, Grib file request tool, and more. Everything a cruiser needs in one free package.   You can also download the latest drivers for the Pactor IIusb modems.

System Requirements

Some boats inherit equipment that is intended for use at shore based Ham stations. While it is true that there are many ways to implement HF SSB communications, the simplest way is to buy the equipment that is focused on marine radio. As stated before, marine radio equipment is usually much easier to use and is marine ready for boats and the environment.

The KISS principal (Keep It Simple Stupid) is the best way to survive cruising. Non-standard marine equipment is not in the KISS category. The cruisers with the most different boxes have the most issues. Another point to consider is that with non-standard installations there is no possibility of getting help from other cruisers. We all need help from time to time. This KISS approach is not the least expensive approach, but it is the best approach for most cruisers.

Unless you are a high tech Radio Geek, to get the most out of HF SSB radio, your system should contain the following equipment for email:

1. HF SSB Marine radio
2. Automatic Antenna tuner that is recommended for your HF SSB radio
3. Antenna
4. Radio Frequency Grounding System separate from boat ground
5. Pactor Modem, with a USB connection.
6. Laptop computer
7. Ferrite cores on all cables to and from the radio, antenna tuner (except the antenna lead), Modem, and computer.
8. Airmail Software
9. Sailmail and/or Winlink account

There are a few other add-ons that are found such as noise canceling (DSP) speakers, microphones, headsets, etc. but if the extra parts are integrated into the basic system above, your system will be as easy as possible to use.

Always make sure you can send and receive messages using the computer, modem, and radio prior to getting underway.

Getting started with Winlink email

Hardware for Winlink Email

The type of modem selected to use with the HF SSB transceiver will determine the connections required between the radio and the computer.   If you have issues in getting connected with email, the Airmail Primer available free at Sailmail.com provides very good instructions, troubleshooting tools, and software updates for most Pactor modems.

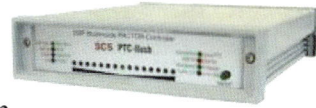

There is new software called WINMOR that is free and allows the user to eliminate the Pactor Modem and use a sound card and PC to communicate with Winlink.   This system works OK, but is not for the typical cruiser as it requires a lot more attention and configuring than does the Pactor modem. The cost for setting up the WINMOR method will run you about $500. The cost for a Pactor solution will start at approximately $1000.   I do not recommend WINMOR for the typical Cruisers.   Hams that go cruising and do not mind tweaking the system to make it work may find the reduced cost worth the extra trouble keeping their email working.

Be sure to install ferrite cores on both ends of all cables going to and from the transceiver, modem and the computer.

If ferrite cores have not been installed on all cables, you can expect frequent computer lock ups while transmitting.   The amount of radiation back into the boat varies with each boat. In some cases you may need several cores on each cable to keep the computer from locking up.

Download and Use Airmail

Be sure to download all the Airmail modules.   I would also recommend you download both the Ham and Sailmail versions, especially if you are planning on cruising across an ocean.

Wherever you are planning to cruise, check the area ahead of time to make sure you will be able to connect to the email system you are using.

Airmail Icon Definitions

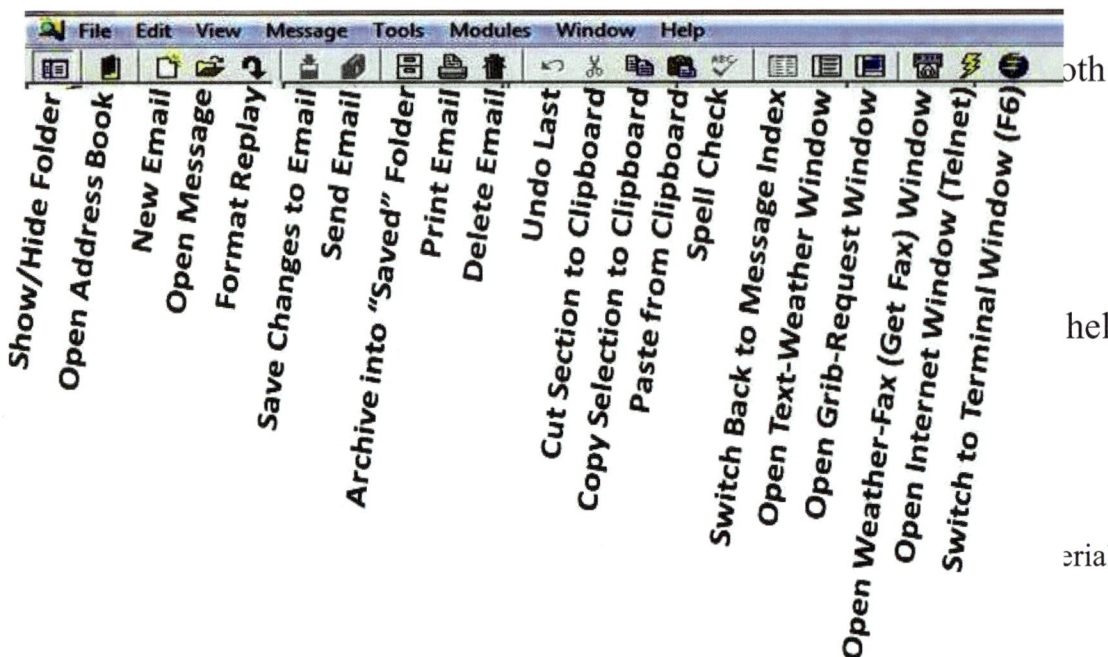

Show/Hide Folder
Open Address Book
New Email
Open Message
Format Replay
Save Changes to Email
Send Email
Archive into "Saved" Folder
Print Email
Delete Email
Undo Last
Cut Section to Clipboard
Copy Selection to Clipboard
Paste from Clipboard
Spell Check
Switch Back to Message Index
Open Text-Weather Window
Open Grib-Request Window
Open Weather-Fax (Get Fax) Window
Open Internet Window (Telnet)
Switch to Terminal Window (F6)

Download Manual: http://www.w7oem.org/wp-content/uploads/2012/03/basic_winlink_2000_training_guide_jun09.pdf

Using Airmail Program with the Internet

The easiest way to establish your Winlink or Sailmail account is to utilize an Internet connection and check for email. If your system is set up properly the internet mode will work. This method will make sure that you have an account (the services recognize your call sign and password) before you start the process of making sure your transmitter and modem work. Some of the Icons are not standard Microsoft Icons. Airmail Icons are defined below.

Process to Setup Winlink Internet mode

1. To get the internet mode working with Airmail your computer must be connected to the internet.
2. Start the Airmail software.
3. Select **Module** then **Internet Access**

47

4. Press the [Settings] button on the popup.

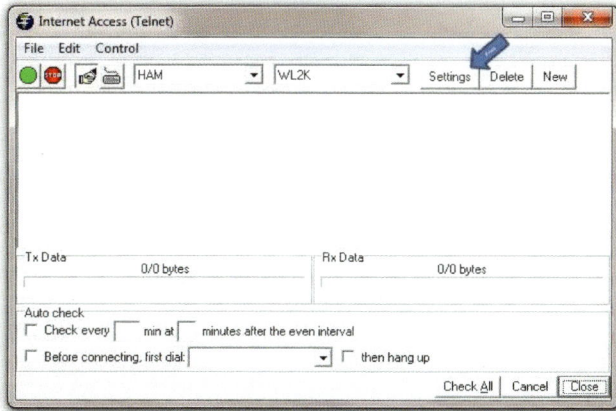

5. The settings should be similar as below and the attached pictures for Winlink.

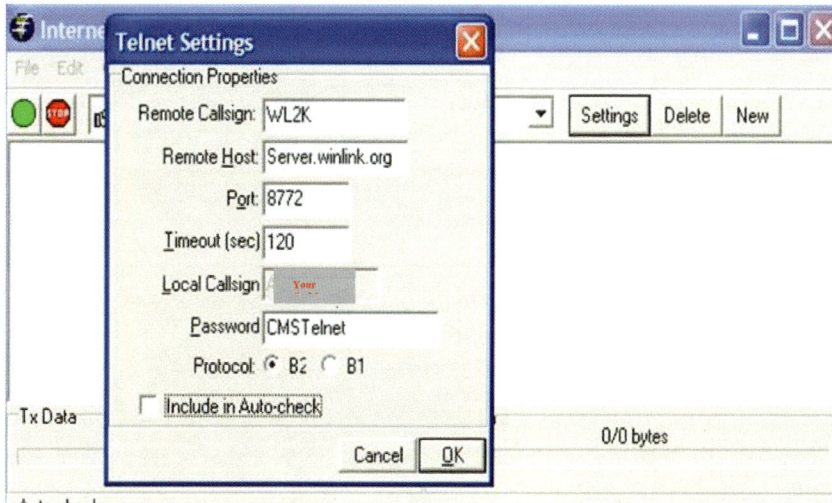

    a. Remote Callsign: WL2K

    b. Remote Host: Server.winlink.org

         Or use: Sandiego.winlink.org; Halifax.winlink.org

    c. Port: 8772

    d. Timeout 120

    e. Local Call sign: Your Ham call sign not the Marine call sign.

    f. Protocol: B2 checked

    g. Un-check Include in Auto-check

6. Press [OK]

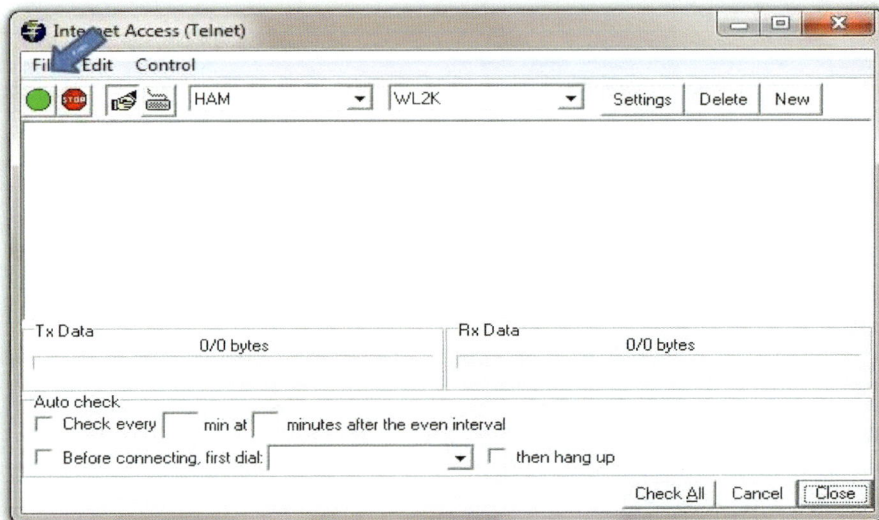

7. Press the green button to start an email replication.
8. When this is working, proceed to testing the HF SSB email via the Pactor Modem.

Using Airmail Program with the HF Radio

Airmail configure was created to be very user friendly. The procedure will vary some depending on the operating system you are using. Since computers have been issued with Windows 7, this procedure is applicable for Windows 7.

Special Note: At the time this book was published, Airmail does not seem to work on Windows 8. It is believed this is as a result of Windows 8 using Aps like phones instead of traditional computer programs.   This is a major change for PPCs. The Icom IC M802 is also used for this procedure as the M802 is used by most Cruisers.   If you are using a Ham radio instead of a Marine radio, this part can be challenging. The procedure also uses the PTC IIpro and PTC IIush as they are both capable of controlling the radio directly. The configuration will also be similar for the new Dragon line of Pactor modems.

1. Connect your Pactor modem to the radio as specified by the modem and radio manuals. Use the premade cables for your radio will make the installation process easy.
    a. There are pre-made cables available for your radio and the type of modem you are using.
    b. With the newer Pactor Modems, most transceivers may be controlled by the modem. A separate cable may also be used to control the radio directly from your computer. I use this method as it seems to work much better, but it does add an additional USB cable that needs to be connected to the computer.
2. Plug your USB cable from the Pactor modem into your computer. The computer should automatically configure a communications port and load the drivers for your computer. If it does not, plug into a different USB port and try again.
    a. If you are using a Pactor Pro modem, a USB to serial converter is also required and the driver for that converter must also be installed separately. Be sure and keep this driver handy as the missing driver can result in not being able to talk to the modem.
3. Go to the Start button, (Microsoft Ball in lower left corner) open and select "Devices and Printers".
4. Go to the bottom of the display and locate the SCS PTCII device.

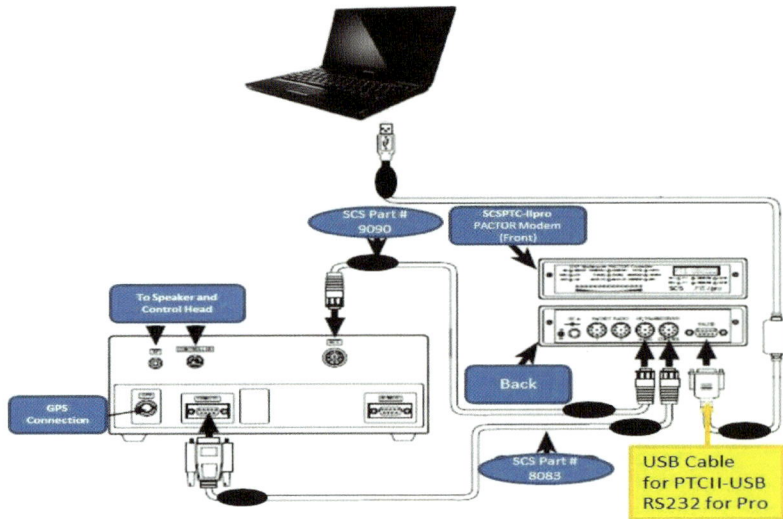

ICOM IC M802 radio with a Pactor PTCII –pro modem and Laptop

5. Do a "right mouse click" on your SCS PTCII device and select "**Properties**".
6. Select "Hardware" folder.
7. Find PTCII device (COMxx) and note it. Com Port # (_____).
8. Close "**Properties**" and "Control Panel".
9. Start the Airmail program.
10. Click on "Tools" and then "Options"
11. Click on "Connection".
12. Select your modem type. E.g. PTC-IIusb or PTC-IIpro

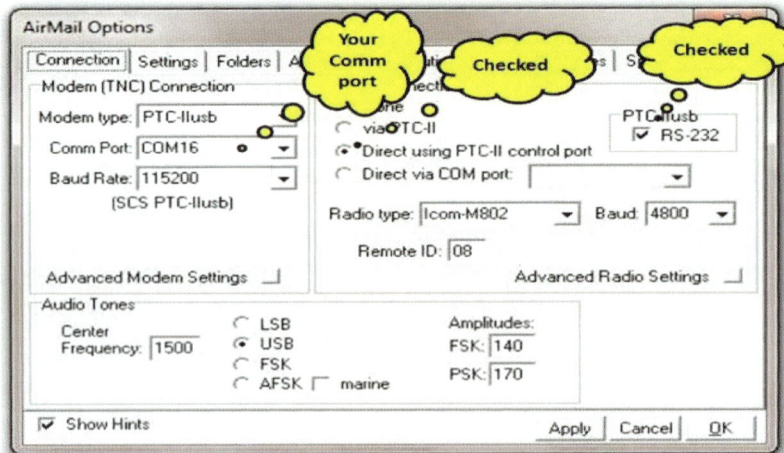

13. Select the "Comm Port:" you found above.

51

14. Make sure the Baud Rate is at "115200" to start with.
15. For Pactor Modems that control the radio frequency and transmit/receive directly such as the PTC-IIusb, PTC-IIpro, and the P4Dragon, you may check "Direct using PTC-II control port" and "PTC-IIusb/RS-232" as in the graphic above.

- If you have a modem that does not control the radio directly or wish to control the radio from the computer, you will have additional cables, serial to USB converters to configure and then the Direct via COM port: must be checked and identified. You will be required to insert the COM port for the radio control link. The COM port can be identified by opening "Devices and Printers" again as above.
- If you have a MAC, and a PTC-IIusb modem, the procedure above may work if you are also running windows 7. You may have to run the MAC at a slower baud rate to make it work.

Receiving and Sending HF SSB Email

Some Cruisers have issues with email. Email on HF SSB is not as simple as when you are connected to the internet. It can be difficult to just get connected to a server. After you are connected, noise can require the server or you to re-transmitting the same information several times until the information is actually transferred.

This all happens automatically via the Airmail program and the Pactor modem coordinating the entire process. It may take a little longer than the internet, but it works great.

1. Open Airmail
2. Create the email(s) by clicking on the Icon that looks like paper with a star in the upper right corner. (3rd Icon from the left at the top of Airmail.)
3. When you have completed writing the email post it to the outgoing mail by clicking on the mailbox Icon. (7th Icon from the left at the top of Airmail.)
4. With your transceiver on and your computer running airmail, note the frequency your radio is on.
5. Select **Module**, then **HF Terminal** on the Airmail program.

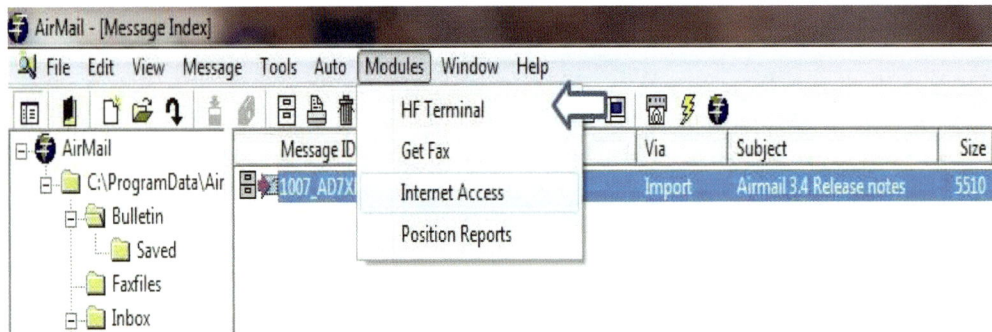

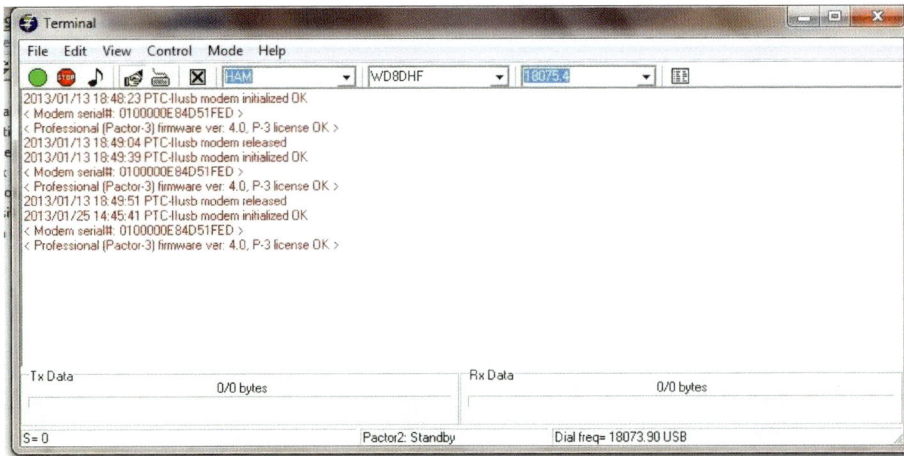

6. After the terminal display identifies it has initialized the modem and the license is OK, the radio indicate a new frequency near the pull down window frequency and may also indicate it is being controlled remotely.
   a. Other radios may use a different format.
   b. The radio should be the listed frequency less 1.5 KHz. The 1.5 KHz is called the offset frequency and is common on email servers.
7. If so, the computer is controlling the transceiver as required.
   a. If not, make sure there is a station and frequency selected in the pull-down windows at the top.
   b. If you have a station and frequency selected, and the radio did/does not change frequency you need to figure out how to get the computer to control the radio.
      i. Check the cables
      ii. Check the configuration options to make sure they reflect the configuration you have.
   c. If the radio's frequency is being controlled go to the next step.
8. Press [F8] on your computer to display the frequency "Propagation" chart.
   a. OR select "View" and then "Propagation (F8)" via the menu.

b. If Propagation does popup, you may be missing or have the wrong Icepac propagation program files. You may also be missing other modules so get a complete download and start over.

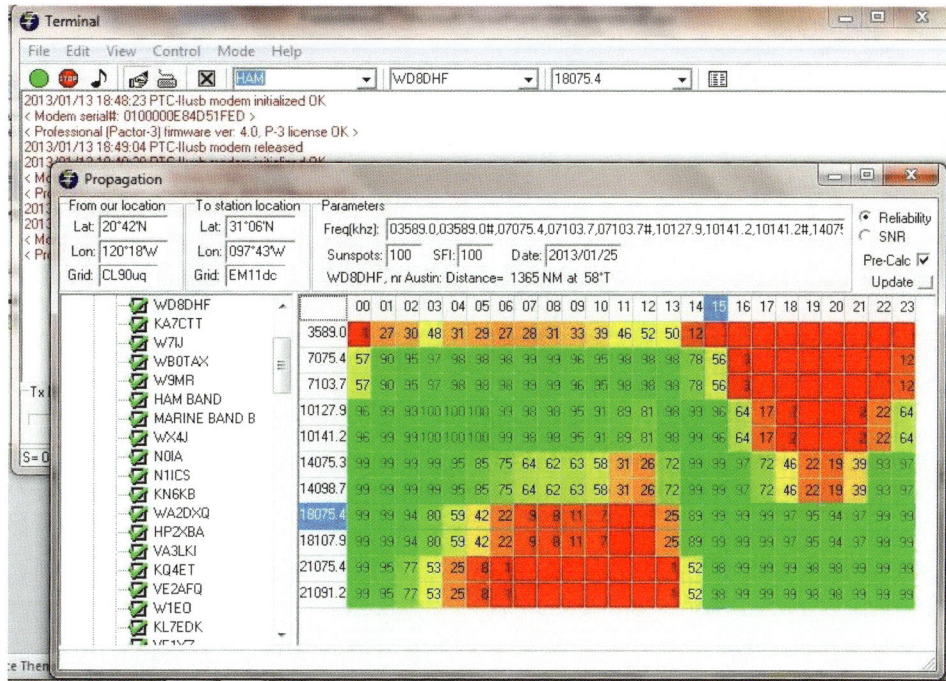

9. When the chart comes up, make sure the correct Latitude and Longitude are displayed in the **From our location** section.

10. The best stations for your location should be at the top of the list. However, it may not be the best, so you may have to do some comparison with other stations to make sure you have the best frequency for your location.

    a. Look for a frequency that is indicating 100% reliability for your UTC time. (The time is marked at the top in UTC with a dark blue coloring of the hour block.)

    b. Note which frequencies are at 100% then change the display to SNR by clicking on "SNR" in the upper right corner of the display.

    c. Note the frequencies that were at 100% when you were in the "Reliability" mode and select the frequency with the largest SNR number.

11. You can use the pull down window on the transmit terminal to select the station and the frequency or double click in the "Propagation" display on the frequency (on the left side of the propagation chart.)

12. Listen to see if you can hear others getting mail.

    a. Don't start until it is clear.

b. If you can hear others getting email, you should be able to get email when they are done. Sometimes it can be useful to look at a few 100% frequencies to make sure you can hear someone.

13. Press the green button on the "Terminal" display to start email retrieval.
   a. The transmitter should be going back and forth between **RX** and **TX** during the process.
   b. The pop up display will add a text line that indicates the present time and date it is calling the selected station on and the specified frequency in KHz.

14. If you cannot connect with the server, try another frequency and/or station. And another and another until you get connected and replicate your email.

The transceiver will continue cycling back and forth until all the emails are sent and retrieved from the server.

There is a status bar at the bottom of the Airmail display that shows progress and if it understood the last received information. Green is yes and red is no!

Note to Cruisers*: The Propagation chart is a best guess and not the only story behind HF radio communications.   There are always things going on that the propagation program is not aware of while it is calculating the best solution.   For example, heavy solar flares, storms, high noise levels in your marina etc.   Calculations for the best station are based on the distance between your station and the email station only.*

When your email is complete be sure and Press "**F**" key and the "**9**" key to get back to High Power.

In the Sea of Cortez email seems to work best early morning and in the evening. That does not mean others do not connect mid-day.

If you cannot get your email working, send me a note or check with another boat in your harbor to see how their email is working and what stations/frequency they are using successfully.

Weather and Wind Information

You select the type of report, make the request, send the request and as per the request the information will be returned.

While weather and wind information may be obtained on the HF SSB Nets, you can also set up a download, via Airmail to provide almost any kind of weather information.

Within the Airmail program, you may request using "SailDocs", Grib files, and

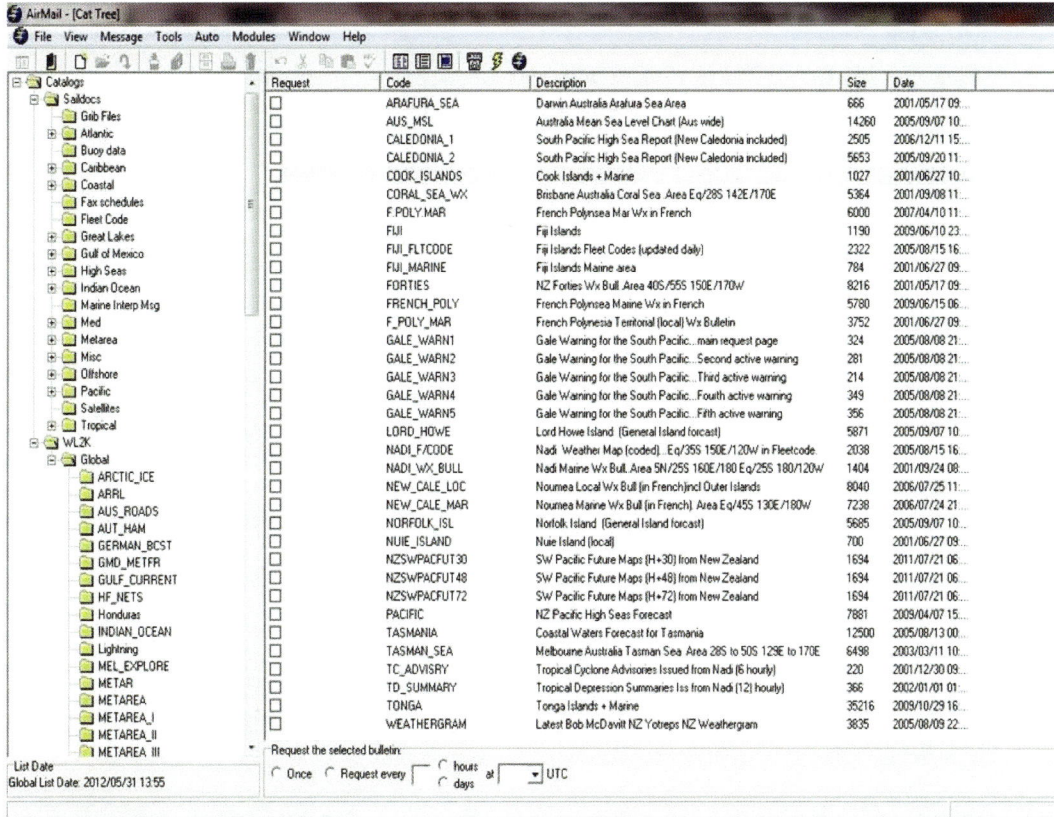

Inquiries.

To get a picture or text information from SailDocs you first have to select the information you want and create a message by selecting the SailDocs. Now clicking on the choices in the "Request the selected Bulletin (at the bottom center of the display) to define how often you want to receive the document.

Use the "Close Button at the bottom right side to close the request screen. If you Use the "X" (upper right hand corner) to close the screen, your selection will be lost. Closing the request screen will generate a message requesting the document you are requesting and place the request in the Airmail outbox. To get SailDocs to send the information, you must now send and receive emails. The email that was generated and sent will key SailDocs to send you the information at the time and frequency you requested when you filled out the form.

SailDocs will actually send you a picture of a web page including things like NOAA weather and Satellite images while Inquiries will send you text information.

In the Sea of Cortez, Cruisers have a fantastic weather resource on the Sonrisa Net (3968.0 KHz LSB) by the name of Baja Geary. Geary gets up every morning at about 4 AM and prepares a micro weather over for the Sea of Cortez, Riviera, and the Pacific Side of the Baja.

A couple of years ago Geary figured out how to generate a text report of his weather onto a SailDocs document and told us how to request the information. The message would be formatted manually as below.
From: Your Ham Call
To: query@saildocs.com
CC:
Subject: Anything you want. ie: Sonrisa Riviera Forecast
In the body:
sub http://www.sonrisanet.org/Saildocs/Outside.html
or
sub http://sonrisanet.org/Saildocs/Sea.html
or
sub http://sonrisanet.org/Saildocs/Riviera.html
Because this is a subscription you may want to add to the end of one of the above requests. days=(1-30) time=14:30

So for the Sea of Cortez:

sub http://sonrisanet.org/Saildocs/Sea.html days=30 time=14:30

(The time must be set to 1430Z or later to obtain todays weather.)

Inquiries will send back text versions of weather for the requested area.

Make a GRIB File Request
If you send a Grib file request, the SailDocs system will send you back wind predictions for the requested area you.

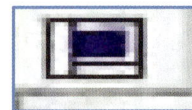

To obtain Grib (Weather information) files:

1. Select the icon: "Open Grib – Request Window"

2. A world map will be displayed
3. Using your mouse: High lite the area you want to receive Grib information about by using your mouse.
   a. The more you select the larger the file will be and the longer it will take to download the file. So only select the information you really need.
   b. As you select an area with your mouse, the area will be marked with a dark colored block drawn on the map.

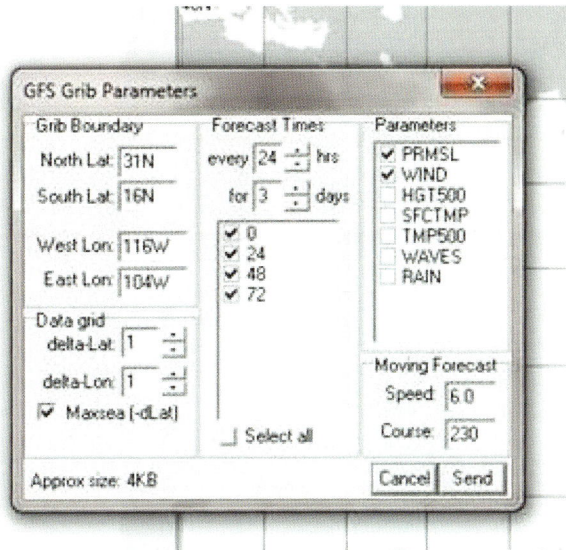

4. At the bottom of the page you can specify a one-time request or multiple-days as well as when you want the Grib file sent.
5. Then Press "Request"
6. A popup window will be displayed which will allow you to hone your selection.
   a. How many days are included in each file,
   b. Latitude and Longitude of request,
   c. Parameters to be downloaded
   d. If you are traveling you can identify your course and speed so that the window moves daily with you.

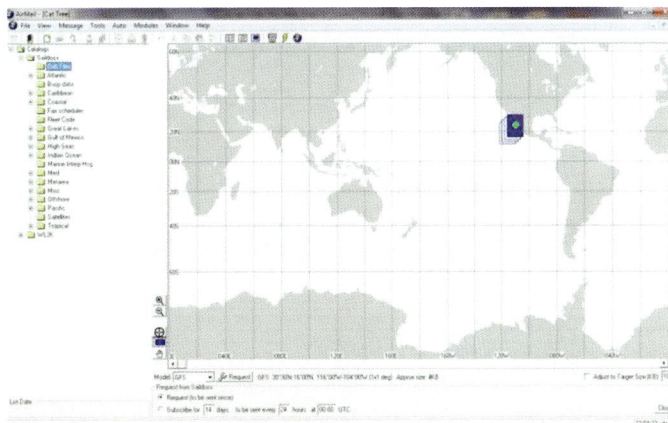

7. Be sure and press "Close" and not the Red "X" in the upper right corner to close and create the request email.
8. An email will be generated:

> To: "Sail Docs" <query@saildocs.com>
> Subject: Saildocs Request
> (In the email)
> sub GFS:29N,18N,115W,105W|-0.5,0.5|0,24..72|PRMSL,WIND|6.0,230,2012122716 Days=10 time=12:00

9. Send the email via Internet or HF SSB modem.
10. After this email is sent, a Grib file will be generated for the box defined by the
    a. latitude and longitudes specified;
    b. with grid separations of 0.5 Latitude and Longitude;
    c. including present day, next day and out to 72 hours;
    d. for PRMSL and Wind data;
    e. with the block moving at 6 knots in the direction of 230 degrees;
    f. As requested at 22Dec2012 at 1600 UTC;
    g. The file will be sent every day for ten days; at 1200 UTC time.
11. Use Airmail to get your email after the time specified.
12. Open the email sent back from SailDocs.
13. Double Click on the GFS Icon/file at the lower left hand side of the email to display your received GRIB file.

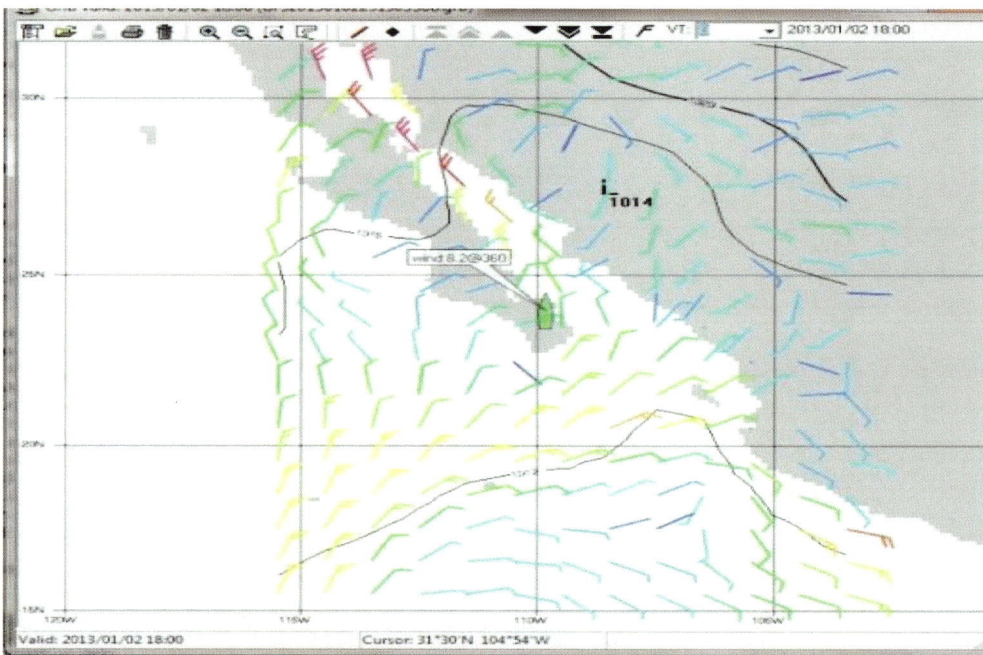

14. Use the pull down at the top right side to look at other days within the document.

Position reporting

The Airmail program will read the position from the Pactor modem if set up within Airmail "Position Report" module. This feature seems to take over the computer in order to multiple position reports. As a result it may be easier to manually enter your position in Airmail.

To send out a position report to various mapping services including your own blog:

Select: "Modules" and then "Position Reports".

Note: If you do not see "Position Reports" in the list of Modules, Open "Tools", "Options", and click on the "Modules" tab. Place a check mark in the "Positions Report" under "Enable Modules"

A pop up window will be provided:

Within the pop up window you may input your position and the time. The time may be input by pressing the "Now". This module also allows you to input local weather information.

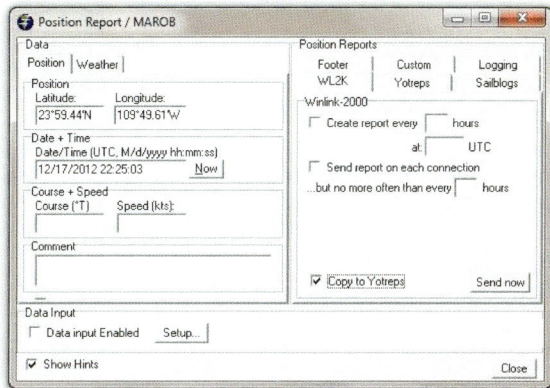

The window also allows you to send the position information to multiple locations. The Ham map is the WL2K tab. Many cruisers also have their positions posted to the Yotreps web site. By checking "Copy to Yotreps" will send to both the WL2K and Yotreps mapping sites. Your position and eventually your track will be recorded on these sites

Both sites are available to the public. If you have a blog, the position information can also be sent there as well. There is some setup involved to send your position and get it posted on your site depending on your web blogs requirements.

7. Text Messages Via HF SSB"

Overview

There are times when you just cannot talk to a fellow cruiser via voice. With voice, we are trying to understand the words and inflections of the calling station. High levels of background noise can make this very challenging.

When you need to get your message out or find out what the weather is going to be, the best alternative to voice communications is digital communications. Digital has a better chance than voice because it is really only looking for ones and zeros in a known format.

Most people are familiar with text messaging on your phone, but did you know that if you use Sailmail or Winlink you have the tools on board to text a fellow cruiser. The process is very simple with only a couple of things to do to change between listening to sending text. This procedure assumes your radio, modem, and Airmail are already set up for use on Sailmail and/or Winlink.

The Process

1. Both the sending and receiving stations must be ready to receive messages.
2. Turn on your radio, Computer, and PACTOR modem.
3. Set the frequency to the desired frequency you are authorized to transmit on.
4. Start the Airmail program
    a. The program you use to do Sailmail and/or Winlink.
    b. Start as if you were getting ready to send and receive email.
5. Using your computer's mouse device, click on "Tools" and then "Dumb Terminal".

a. This will open a window similar to the window you use for Sailmail and/or Winlink.

6. There will be no green start or red stop button.

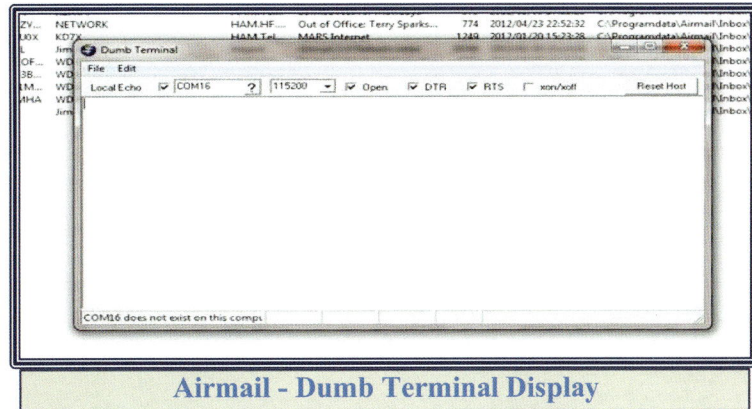

Airmail - Dumb Terminal Display

7. Press "Esc" key to get the Command prompt, "cmd:"
8. To make sure the modems are all using the same tones for marks and spaces
   a. Type: "TO 4" and press the "Enter" key.
9. To increase the power for longer distance communication, you may also se the FSKA command for up to 200. (Recommended range is 60-200)
   a. Type: "FSKA 200" for maximum power.
10. Next start the digital text process communications with the modem. All station(s) wanting to hear and/or send digital information must initiate the process by:
    a. Type "Listen 1" and press "Enter".

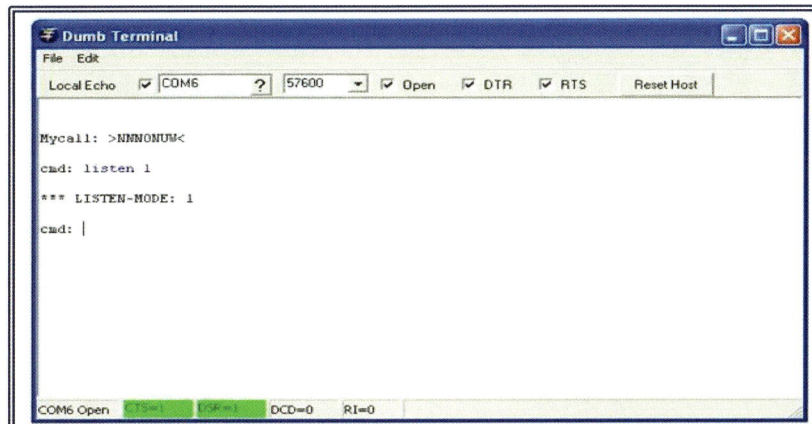

b. Your computer may return with "*** LISTEN-MODE: 1" depending on where the modem was last set.
c. Your modem is now listening.

d. You will now hear any PACTOR modems sending messages on the selected frequency.

e. Press "Esc" key to return to the "cmd:" prompt.

11. To **Send** text to all stations in the listening mode:

a. Type "UN" and press "Enter".

    i. This is the abbreviated version of the UNPRO Command.

b. The computer should display "UNPROTO TRANSMISSION ACTIVE -

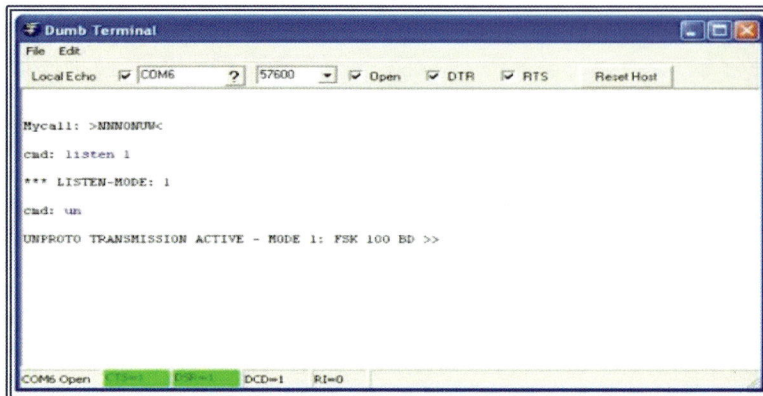

MODE 1: FSK 100 BD >>"

c. The computer display will move to a blank line ready for typing.

d. Type your message(s)

12. If your message is more than 10 lines, I would recommend starting and ending your message with your call sign.

a. Example:

Send a Short Message

XE1-AD7XL   Now is the time for all good men to come to the aid of their Party and that Party is at Geary's house on the 4th of July.   XE1-AD7XL

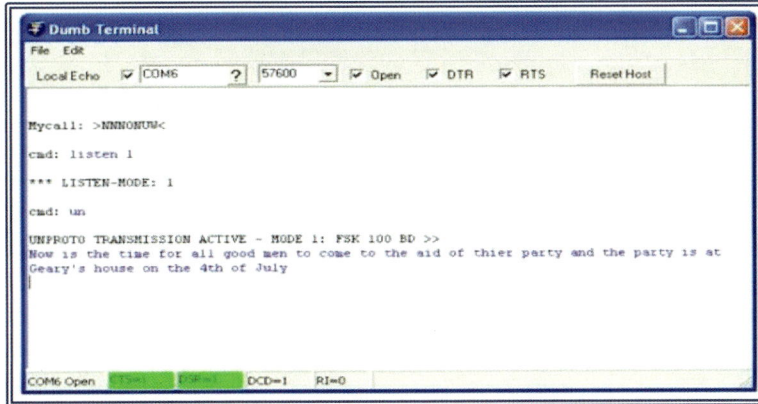

For Long messages

> WDA5497: Now is the time for all good men to come to the aid of their Party and that Party is at Geary's house on the 4th of July.
> For directions of where to go . . . . etc.
> and What to bring . . . . etc.
> And on another subject . . . . etc.
> Kind Regards, Terry: WDA5497

13. When you have completed sending, press and hold "Ctrl" and Press "d" to stop transmitting.

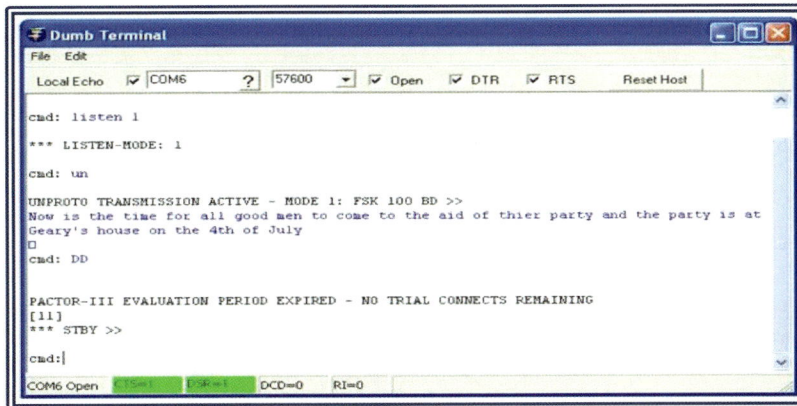

14. Press "Esc" to return to the "cmd:" prompt.
15. It is also possible to do a hard stop on the transmitter as an option. To do a hard stop press "Esc" and then type "DD" and Press "Enter". The Modem will return to the listen mode and display the "cmd:" prompt.
16. If no "cmd:" prompt:
    a. Press "Esc" to return to the "cmd:".
17. When complete, close the terminal window by busing your Mouse Device and clicking on the red "X" in the upper right corner of the Dumb Terminal.

Digital Communications will allow cruisers to get information more accurately and at a longer distance. Most importantly being able to ask those weather questions may increase cruisers overall **Safety at Sea**.

Have fun playing with HF SSB Test Messaging.

See "Quick Reference Guide" Appendix XVI

Cruising Hams Using Marine HF SSB

As a licensed Ham on board a cruising boat, the others on board may look to you for all the communications answers. I have received numerous questions from new Hams about Marine band communications. As a result I have provided a couple of chapters on important items with regard to the Marine radio bands.

You are required to have a "Ships Station License" from your country's communication control organization if you are out of your country. In the United States it is the Federal Communications Commission (FCC). Marine HF SSB radio is considered long range communications and if you have one on board you must have the "Ships Station License" even in your home country.

The "Ships Station License" provides the call sign required to talk on marine bands as well as a Maritime Mobile Service Identity (MMSI) number. To talk on the Marine bands, an Operator permit is also required. If one person has an operator's permit on a boat, others may talk under the licensed person's supervision.

8. What to do in an Emergency

As the Ham on board, others will be looking to you to get help via the radios on board during an emergency situation. If you have an Icom IC M802 the process for getting help is very simple and discussed in detail in another chapter.

If you have an older marine radio or possibly bought a boat and got stuck with a Ham radio you have some preparation that needs to be completed prior to starting cruising.

The first thing to do is get your radio ready by programming all of the emergency calling and working channels into your radio.

The emergency calling frequencies include 2,182.0 KHz, 4,125.0 KHz, 6,215.0 KHz, 8,291.0 KHz, and 12,290.0 KHz.

Make a May Day call when life is at immediate risk or a Pan Pan call when you have a lessor emergency but still anticipate a critical situation is imminent.

Call on one of the emergency frequencies above. If no one responds, go to the next frequency and make a call. While 2182.0 KHz may be a good frequency to use in some locations, it might be better to start with 8,291.0 KHz to maximize the potential locations receiving your call.   However there are no real rules for which channel to use first. If you try them all, someone will probably hear you.

If you have tried all the frequencies and no one has responded, do it again.   You can also try Communications Net frequencies, Ham frequencies and even Airline control frequencies in an emergency.

For a May Day Emergency Call

Mayday, Mayday, Mayday, this is Call Sign _____ (Vessel) _____
Mayday, Mayday, Mayday, this is Call Sign _____ (Vessel) _____
Mayday, Mayday, Mayday, this is Call Sign _____ (Vessel) _____

For a Pan Pan Emergency Call

PAN PAN, PAN PAN, PAN PAN this is Call Sign _____ (Vessel)_____
PAN PAN, PAN PAN, PAN PAN this is Call Sign _____ (Vessel)_____
PAN PAN, PAN PAN, PAN PAN this is Call Sign _____ (Vessel)_____

After you have made contact with the station responding to your call, they may ask you to shift to an equivalent working frequency channel.

Working channels are **duplex**, meaning the transmit frequency and the receive frequency assignment are different. This allows the shore station to listen to everything you are saying even if they are trying to talk. Most people can get very excited and ramble on in an emergency.   The shore station will hear you talking and can wait to transmit until after you have stopped. The station will probably record your transmission.

If you made contact for a May Day call on 8.291MHz, the contacted station may ask you to go to the 8MZ working channel, e.g. RX 8764.0 and TX 8,240.0 KHz. See Appendix VX for Coast Guard / International emergency calling and working channels. Be sure and pre-program all the emergency hailing and working channels into your transceiver.

It is difficult to program a frequency in an emergency, especially a duplex frequency!

Make sure everyone on board knows how to make a distress call on all types of equipment on your boat.   (VHF, HF, DSC applicable radios, EPIRB, and even the Sat Phone)   The captain and/or the licensed Ham operator may be busy during a distress situation or even the reason for the distress situation, so training in advance is the best approach to a successful outcome.

9. Using Digital Selective Calling

Emergency Calls – Made Simple with DSC

Digital Selective calling is an important part of modern Marine HF SSB radios. This feature has been defined detailed in my other books with additional information on my web site. DSC is such an important feature for cruisers and not many cruisers are aware of the advantages of DSC. I use every chance possible to enlighten the fleet about HF SSB DSC.

Search and Rescue
Search and Rescue (SAR) stations around the world monitor the emergency digital frequencies used for DSC distress, urgent, and ship safety calls.

When you send a DSC distress or urgent call on a DSC capable HF SSB radio, the SAR stations, possibly even around the world, get a loud alarm in their control facility.

On a DSC capable radio like the Icom IC M802, the distress DSC calling feature does the work for you. The process for DSC distress calling will be explained in detail later in this chapter.

Interface with Commercial Vessels
A United Nations agency called the International Maritime Organization (IMO) established the need for a program called Global Maritime Distress and Safety System (GMDSS) in 1979. GMDSS is now required on all large commercial vessels over 300 tons.

GMDSS Required Equipment
- A VHF radio installation capable of transmitting DSC on channel 70, and radiotelephony on channels 16, 13 and 6.
- One SART if under 500 GRT, 2 SARTs if over 500 GRT.
- Two portable VHF transceivers for use in survival craft if under 500 GRT, three if over 500 GRT.
- NAVTEX receiver, if the ship is engaged on voyages in any area where a NAVTEX service is provided.
- Inmarsat EGC receiver, if the ship is engaged on voyages in any area of Inmarsat coverage where MSI services are not provided by NAVTEX or HF NBDP.
- 406 MHz EPIRB
- MF radio capable of transmitting and receiving on emergency DSC frequency 2187.5 kHz and voice frequency 2182.0 kHz.

- DSC watch keeping receiver operating on the DSC emergency frequency 2187.5 kHz.

In a few words, GMDSS is an internationally required system for vessels over 300 tons that includes DSC HF and VHF radios, Satellite systems and other equipment with established communication protocols. The GMDSS is used to increase safety and make it easier to rescue distressed ships, boats and aircraft.

While a cruiser is not required to have a GMDSS, your link into the GMDSS world is via your DSC capable equipment. When you make a HF DSC distress call, it will not only reach the SAR shore stations, but more importantly the call will reach commercial vessel that could be just over the horizon.

It is important to remember that GMDSS vessels (large commercial vessels greater than 300 tons) have doctors, drugs, people, and other potential needs that can save your life. As per the law of the sea, they will help you in a distress situation.

If your vessel is sinking, a SAR station 1,000 miles away may not provide much help. Whereas your HF SSB radio will transmit a ground wave out up to 150 miles in all directions. VHF DSC calls are typically less than twenty miles in all directions. Both VHF and HF DSC distress calls are worth a try in an emergency. A satellite phone call home (or to a SAR station) can result in help arriving many hours or even days later.

During a friends sail to Hawaii from Baja California he got violently sick and was facing death. They made a call out, contacted a commercial vessel. The commercial vessel came to their location with a doctor and drugs on board to keep my friend alive. Prior to contacting the commercial vessel, my friend had already told his crew that when he died, enter the details into the ships log with the date and time he died and throw his body overboard. VHF DSC is great and HF DSC is even better.

The EPIRB is easy and best known distress tool. If you are far off shore it could take even days to get help on site. If my boat is sinking, I may not have a day and do not want to spend a few days in a life raft. So my priority list for communications devices is based on time to arrive and not time to respond via voice on the radio. There could be vessels at or over the horizon or maybe even within a 100 miles that could be at your location within hours.

So my order of priority for telling the world I am in trouble is as follows:

1. EPIRB – Let Long Range Know
2. VHF DSC – Call Looking for Local
3. HF DSC Call – Local & Long Range

4. HF Mayday Call – Local & Long Range
5. Sat Phone Call – Long Range
6. HF Nets – Long Range
7. HF Airline Control Nets – Long Range

Be sure and work out your priority order. Your priority order should be based on where you are cruising.

What Happens on an Icom IC M802 for a Distress Calls

The Icom IC M802 is an amazing unit for the dollars.   While there are cruisers that say the M802 HF SSB radio is very expensive, the next higher priced DSC radio has a price tag that is approximately $1000 higher than a typical IC M802.

Pressing the Distress button is probably the best way to do a distress call. There is also a menu driven distress call that allows you to add the nature of the call.   Instead of fumbling with the menu in an emergency, just press the distress button for approximately 5 seconds and let the IC M802 do its thing.

What happens when I press the M802 Distress Button?
By pressing and hold the distress button, the IC M802 begins its distress calling process. And it is a process with many automatic steps to help the operator complete a distress call in the easiest way possible while maximizing the potential stations receiving the call.

Initially the radio broadcasts a digital message on the 8MHz emergency DSC frequency. The radio sends your position data, time of call, and your MMSI number within the digital message that is sent. (The message is set up to also include the situation if a menu driven distress call was sent.) After the DSC message has been sent, the radio automatically shifts to the international 8 MHz voice emergency frequency. This will allow the operator to make a voice May Day call and hopefully connect with a monitoring SAR station. The only indication that the radio is waiting for you to do a May Day Call is that the display changes from "**Distress Calling**" to "**Distress <Wait for ACK>**".   Then make the Voice May Day Call.

After 4-5 minutes the IC M802 shifts to the 12 MHz DSC emergency calling frequency and re-transmits the same digital message. After the digital message is sent, the IC M802 will shift to the 12 MHz voice emergency calling frequency to allow the operator to complete the Mayday call on the 12 MHz emergency calling frequency.

The radio will repeat the process for 16 MHz, then 2 MHz, then 6 MHz, and then start all over again at 8 MHz. This process will continue until a distress acknowledgement is received or the operator presses and holds the call cancel button. If someone responds to your voice May Day call, be sure and press "Call/Cancel" so the M802 does not automatically change to the next frequency.

See the flow chart on the next page to see a graphical representation for the big picture of how it all works.

Overview:
1. Press Distress
2. M802 goes to "**Distress Calling**" on 8,414.5 KHz
3. Watch for the display to go to "**Distress <Wait for ACK>**"
4. Display changes to "**Distress <Wait for ACK>**" and 8,291.0 KHz
5. Make the Mayday Call until the display shifts again.
6. M802 goes to "**Distress Calling**" on 12,577.0 KHz
7. Watch for the display to go to "**Distress <Wait for ACK>**"
8. Display changes to "**Distress <Wait for ACK>**" and 12,290.0 KHz
9. Repeats the above steps for 16 MHz, 2 MHz, 4 MHz, 6 MHz and back to 8MHz. The M802 will continue this process until a Distress Acknowledgement or the "Call/Cancel" button is held for 3 seconds.

**** If you contact someone during a May Day, press Call Cancel to stop the M802 from automatically going to the next frequency.****

Distress Call Flow on an Icom IC M802

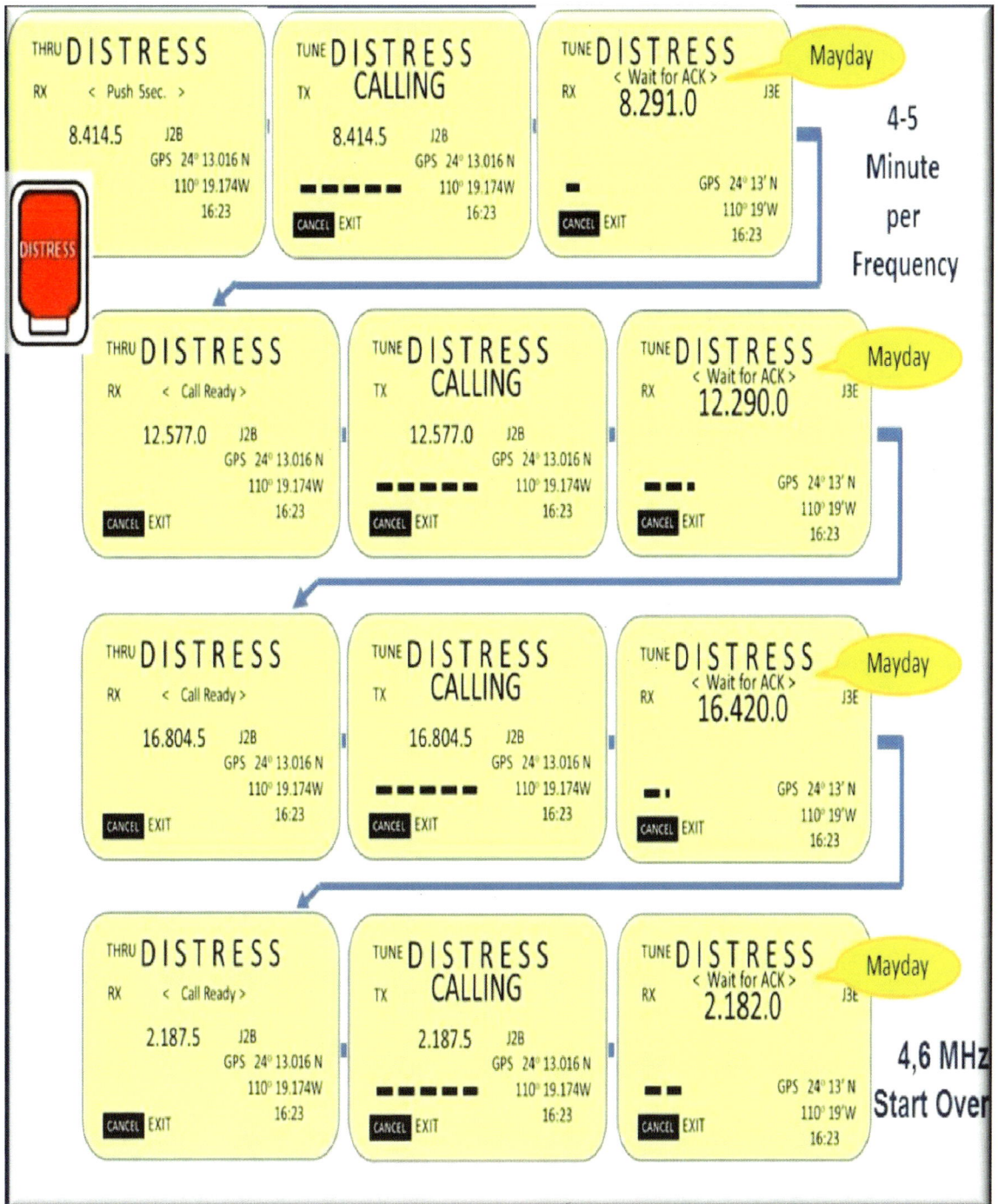

Urgent Calls

The next level of priority communications is "Pan". Similar to the Mayday communications, you should not try to hail other vessels when you hear "PAN PAN, PAN PAN, PAN PAN".

Within the DSC system, an Urgency DSC call is similar to a voice "PAN PAN" call. To send an urgent message to an individual location or all ships is similar. I would recommend all ships.

Urgent Calls are used when safety of personnel is in danger, but not immediate. For example, you are adrift because your vessel is out of gas, the engine will not start, or medical transport is required.

Ship Safety Calls

The next level of emergency communications is the safety call, "Security" pronounced "Securitay". The Coast guard will often identify notification of storm warnings and other messages that may affect the ability of vessels to maintain safe marine navigation following a call of "Securitay, Securitay, Securitay".

Vessels often report logs in the water and other hazards via a Security call. Within the DSC system the equivalent digital call is called a Safety Call.

All of the above emergency communications calls come into the IC M802 via the DSC Emergency Reception Antenna (DERA) and the dedicated emergency receiver within the Icom IC M802.

10. Voice Communication on Marine Radio

Ship to Ship Channels

There are many frequencies that may be used for voice and digital communications within the Marine bands. A simplistic approach for frequency identification that cruisers use is to use what I call the alpha channels. They have shortcut names for frequencies that include the MHz band and an alpha character. Examples are 2A, 2B, , , 4A, , , 8B, , , , 25G. While these frequencies are not the only ship to ship voice channels available on HF Marine band HF SSB, they keep it simple for a cruiser with a few frequencies in each band. Saying "Meet me on 8 Bravo" will result in everyone knowing exactly where to tune the radio. If Net Control transmits a frequency change and says, "let's go to 8, 2, 9, 7 Kilo Hertz" instead of "8 Bravo", this would result in requests for frequency repeats and probably people lost to the net during the shift.

There are no tricks to using these channels. They are simply HF SSB frequencies assigned to the Marine bands for voice communications between vessels. The channels are all upper sideband (USB) and separated by at least 3KHz.

A matrix of these frequencies is included in Appendix XIV. It is recommended that these channels be programmed into your HF SSB radio, sequentially. Programming the channels sequentially make it easy to find and change to the next sequential alpha channel frequency if the planned frequency is in use. Be sure and label them with the shortcut name so that if a friend says lets meet on 4B, you can go there without looking up the frequency. Also, leave some spaces to program an additional ship to ship channel for those friends that insist on doing it the hard way.

These frequencies are Marine band frequencies, so be sure and use your Ship Station License call sign and not your Ham call sign.

Marine Nets

There are nets that allow vessels with just a "Ships Station License" to check in with and those that allow only Ham licensed person to check in. **In an emergency you can use them all!**

Pacific Coast Nets on the Marine channels include:

Name	Time UTC	Frequency	Mode
Picante	13:30	6212.0KHz	USB*
Amigo	14:00	8122.0KHz	USB*
Southbound	00:55	8122.0KHz	USB*

* All Marine band communications are Upper Sideband.

The Amigo and Southbound Nets also have alternate frequencies when there is a conflict, Interference, or when they desire to shorten the communications range. At the time of this book, the Amigo uses 8A and 8B as the alternate frequencies and 4B as the short range frequency. Southbound also uses 4B as the short range frequency after they long-range net.

Pre-program the primary and alternate frequencies for the nets where you plan to cruise. Program the channels in order of the time of day the net occurs for ease of use. E.g. Channel 101 is my first net in the morning and 102 is the next net in the money.

Routine DSC Calls

HF SSB is Different than VHF DSC Calling
The main difference for DSC calling on HF SSB vs. DSC calling on VHF is that HF SSB radio covers a much broader range of frequencies. Digital calling band will be similar to the band used to complete a voice call. The best band for a voice call is dependent on the distance between the two stations making the call at the time of day the call is made. Likewise, HF SSB DSC must use the same band for the digital call.

Typically HF SSB DSC calling is completed using six frequencies, one in each of the 2, 4, 6, 8, 12, and 16 MHz HF bands. On VHF radios, only one frequency is used, VHF channel 70.

Because it is necessary to use different frequencies for calling, the radio must scan and listen for incoming calls on six different frequencies. For the Icom IC M802 this is called the DSC Watch. DSC Watch uses the normal antenna and not the DERA antenna to listen for the incoming calls.

To receive DSC calls on an IC M802 radio, the radio must be on and in "DSC Watch". On the IC M802 DSC Watch is started by pressing the DSC button on the left side of the controller.

As shipped, the IC M802 is set up for one simplex 2 MHz ship to ship calls and five duplex, ship to shore call channels. The reason for this programming is probably that commercial ships using DSC calling typically have shore locations they contact. As cruisers we only call ship to ship and do not need the ship to shore duplex feature.

There is a procedure on my web site to modify the programming of the IC M802 to allow for ship to ship calls on all six frequencies. By implementing this change, it will allow DSC calls between cruisers on all six frequencies that will extend the potential range of DSC calling for cruisers. To enhance your IC M802 download the procedure at:
http://www.made-simplefor-cruisers.com/ic-m802-2

The procedure is called "**DSC Upgrade for Cruisers**". Both radios (caller and called radios) must be programmed the same to extend the calling range otherwise you will be limited to the 2MHz calling frequency.

DSC Calling to Other Stations
Digital Selective Calling (DSC) is available on a few modern radios. The calling radio sends out a digital signal on one of six calling frequencies. Dependent on the type of call, the radio will then shift frequencies to the Traffic Frequency on both or all radios for a group call. The call is made from one MMSI to another MMSI. If you have a red distress button on your radio, VHF or HF you are supposed to have your MMSI number programmed into the radio.

Be sure and put your MMSI number on your sailing cards so everyone knows your new phone number.

If you are using an Icom IC M802 Marine Radio, to receive or make calls you must first place the radio in the DSC Watch mode by pressing the "DSC" button on the left side of the control head.

Icom radios prior to the Icom IC M802 have no DSC capability.

If you have a DSC equipped radio, you can make a call to a friend using the DSC. The IC M802 scans 6 frequencies in the DSC Watch mode that may be used to establish a call to another location.

Keys to Making a DSC Call

1. An individual or group call may be made with a few strokes of the keys.
2. The Maritime Mobile Service Identity (MMSI) number is used as the phone number for an individual call and a unique number programmed in all radios within a group will cause them all to ring when a group call is sent out.
3. The Icom operating manual or my "Icom IC M802 Made Simple for Cruisers" and "Icom IC M802 Starting from Scratch" books provide all the details for making a DSC call to a friend.

DSC Calling is only available within the Marine Bands.

When making a DSC call, select the same frequency range for calls and traffic (voice communications). E.g. Pick a 2MHz voice frequency if you are calling on 2 MHz, 4MHz voice frequency if you are calling on 4 MHz, etc.

If you do not make contact, make another call on another frequency band. E.g. 2MHz did not work so try 4 MHz and then 6MHz.

Group calls can also be made when a common group number is programmed into the radio by both or the many parties of the group. All members of the group must have the unique number programmed into the DSC address book and be in DSC Watch to receive the call. After accepting the call each member of the group's radios will automatically shift to the traffic frequency.

If you have an Icom IC M802, consider getting a copy of my "Icom IC M802 Made Simple for Cruisers" for simplified operating procedures including DSC. If you are planning to install a new M802, look at "Icom IC M802 Starting from Scratch" as it will walk you through, planning, purchasing, licensing, installation, testing and includes the operating procedures from the other book. It also includes a section on setting up HF SSB email using a Pactor Modem.

Marine Operator Calls

WLO and KLB Radio
In the US there is only one remaining company that provides Marine Operator services. The company call signs are WLO radio and KLB radio. They have ITU duplex Marine frequency channels assigned.

It is recommended that you program these ITU channels in sequentially in the user channel area. WLO radio does a basic weather report on the hour for approximately 15 minutes. While the weather report is not adequate for mariners, it does provide a beacon so that you can determine what the actual propagation is between WLO radio and your station. See Appendix VI for frequency assignments.

When you want to make a call, you listen for the weather report at the top of the hour and dial between the ITU channels quickly to determine the best frequency between you and the marine operator.

It is recommended that cruisers creating an account with WLO radio so that in the event you need to make a call, you will not have to read your credit card over the air. WLO radio is also another option during an emergency situation. There is someone at WLO radio 7X24 and they will help you even without an account.

Marine Calls from Friends and Families are Waiting
At the end of the weather broadcast, the operator typically states that the weather is complete, they have calls waiting for various vessels and that they are now taking calls. So if you have family that plan to call you, you need to monitor the top of the hour weather report so that you will know they have called. The operator will initiate the call the same as normal as the call is not actually on hold.

Making a Marine Call
The process to make a Marine Operator call is simple.

1. Go to the ITU channels on the hour and search for the strongest frequency by checking each of their assigned frequencies.
2. After the weather is completed the operator will say we are now taking calls.
3. Call out WLO radio, WLO radio; this is Sailing Vessel Good Ship WBA1234 on channel 1, 2, 1, 2. (For ITU channel 1212).
4. Keeping in mind that there is probably only one operator that is monitoring for calls for both WLO and KLB stations. So be patient! You may have to call back several times before the operator actually returns your call.
5. When the operator acknowledges your station, they may ask you to repeat your vessel and call sign.

6. When the call is initiated, the person on the other end will be talking on a phone. (Duplex send and receive at the same time)
7. WLO radio is also duplex.
8. We are on Duplex Frequencies, but our Microphone, Push to Talk button, dictates whether we are talking or listening. As a result saying over at the end of your statement will inform the other party you have completed your talking and are no longer transmitting. Basically you are telling them that you will now be listening for what they have to say.
9. When you complete your call and the other party has hung up, call the WLO radio operator back to tell them you are clear with something like: "WLO Radio, WLO Radio this is Sailing Vessel Good Ship and our call is complete."
10. When the operator acknowledges the completion of your call, end your communication with something like: "This is WBA1234 and we are clear".

11. Using Marine Frequency email

Sailmail

Sailmail is a subscription service that is provided internationally for cruisers and other vessels. In some parts of the cruising world such as the South Pacific, the coverage for Sailmail is much better than Winlink. Some Hams also use Sailmail or use Sailmail instead of Winlink as a result of Sailmail's excellent availability. Be sure and find out what email service will provide the best service for your vessel before you head to the area.

The setup on Sailmail is basically the same as the setup for Winlink. However, the frequencies used to replicate your mail, report positions, obtain Grib files, etc. are Marine band frequencies and are all upper sideband (USB).

Since the setup of Sailmail being similar to Winlink, the process is not repeated. You must establish an account with Sailmail prior to completing the setup of your system. Your Ship Station License call sign will be your Sailmail name. Sailmail will provide you with a password to enter when setting up your account.

The easiest thing to do first is to get Internet email mode working. That will make sure that you have in fact an account, the services recognize your name and password.

1. To get the internet mode working with Airmail your computer must be connected to the internet.
2. Start the Airmail software.
3. Select **Module** then **Internet Access**
4. Press the [Settings] button on the popup.

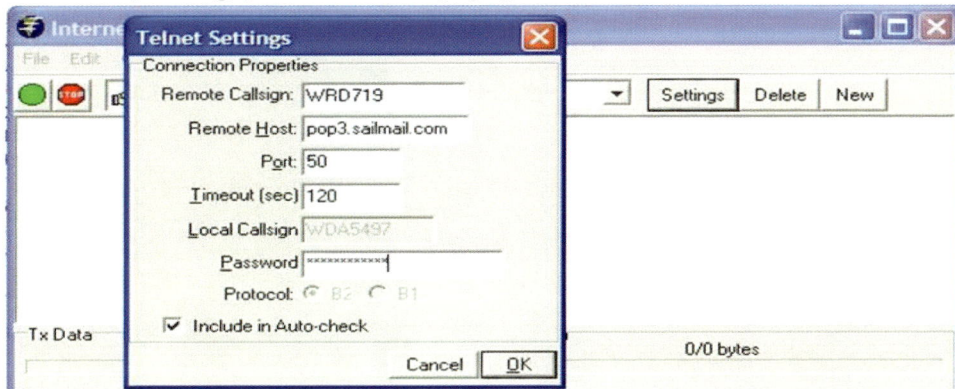

5. The settings should be similar to the picture above and the text below for a Sailmail account.

a. Sailmail
   i. Remote Callsign: WRD719
   ii. Remote Host: pop3.sailmail.com
   iii. Port: 50
   iv. Timeout 120
   v. Local Call sign: Your Marine call sign, not your Ham call sign.
   vi. Protocol: B2 checked
   vii. Check Include in Auto-check

If you have a Sailmail account and it will not let you replicate via the internet or HFSSB, the issue is probably the password setting so re-check your Sailmail account.

Before trying Sailmail with your HF SSB, go to the "Options" popup under the "Tools" and check your settings to make sure the assigned password and your call sign is listed.

* Maintenance*

12. System Routine Maintenance

Indicators

We operate our HF SSB radios in a tough environment when cruising. Like other boat parts, we get corrosion on connections and wires that can fray from rubbing. The sun can also destroy standoffs and the wire's insulation that is exposed.

Take a look at your system frequently and look for the green corrosion, broken tie wraps, and frayed wires.

When using the radio, make sure the tune indicator remains with a tune indication throughout your transmissions. If you have a radio that indicates when the SWR is high, watch for a momentary high SWR indication when you are transmitting.

If you have a power indicator, make sure it is representing the power output indication you expect. The output power will vary with the loudness of your voice into the microphone.

If you are having trouble hearing or reaching other radio stations, that is also a good indication that you need to take a hard look at your system. While talking into the microphone, the power will fluctuate with your voice. To check the total power out, change the mode to FSK (Frequency Shift Keying). This will result in a tone at a 100% modulation level being transmitted when the microphone push to talk switch is depressed. Press the push to talk switch to measure the power.

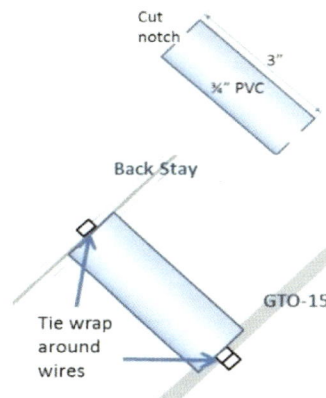

System Checks

When your HF SSB system is installed, record the initial power and reflected power readings on each band. It is a good investment for a cruiser is a power meter that will measure forward and reflected power.

There is an Excel spreadsheet on my web site under the communications tab used to record your initial readings and calculate the actual Standing Wave Ratio (SWR). On the same page there is a basic procedure you may follow to use a basic power/reflected power meter to check your system.
(*Many thanks to Chris an Ann-Marie on S/V Starship for building the log sheet for us all to use.*)

It is recommended that you measure the forward and reflected power at least every couple of years and compare it to the original measurements.

As corrosion starts to develop it will impact your system reflected power and SWR. When SWR goes up find the corrosion and clean it to get your system working its best again.

Cleaning Spots

Cruisers and their radio equipment live in an environment that is very corrosive.   In addition, the RF currents and fields tend to enhance the corrosion.

There are many products available to clean contacts as well as other products that may be used to coat the contacts after corrosion is removed.   RF connections can also be covered with volcanizing tape to help reduce corrosion.   However, just because it has tape on it does not mean it is corrosion free. So cut the tape off and inspect, clean as necessary then re-tape the connection if your SWR starts to increase.

General Inspections
Inspect your radio system cabling for frayed or warn cables and repair or replace as required.   Clean the area where the transceiver is located and make sure the unit has good air flow.

Back Stay Antennas
The connection of the High Voltage cable to the backstay is always an issue for corrosion. When this point gets corroded it can even eat through the wire.   A poor connection could damage the transmitter output.   Fold the wire and solder to maximize the surface area of the antenna connection when repairing the connection after corrosion has damaged the end.

Fiberglas Pole Antennas Connections

This type of antenna has a bolt and nut that will corrode and should be cleaned annually. As with the backstay, if this connection is poor, you will not be able to communicate at your best and could also damage the transmitter output if the connection opens up.

Antenna Tuner Connections

Clean both the antenna and ground connections on the Antenna tuner.

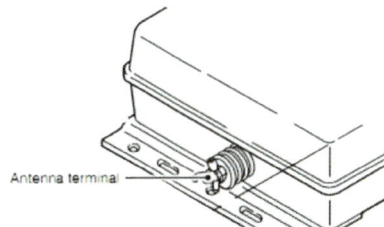

Antenna terminal

Ground Connections

The RF ground system is also another source of corrosion. Annual inspection and cleaning of connections and plates can help maintain your HF SSB system as one of the better systems among cruisers.

Coaxial Connectors

The connectors that connect the transceiver and the antenna tuner are called UHF connectors (PL259 and SO239 plugs and connectors). These connectors can also corrode over time even when they are covered with Volcanizing tape and provide losses to your transmitters output. This is also true on your fixed Marine VHF radios. When SWR is increasing; inspect, clean, and re-seal with tape again with volcanizing tape the connections with vulcanizing tape.

Clean and Shiny works

Snap on Ferrite Cores in Place

Make sure that the snap on Ferrite cores are still tightly coupled to the cables. If the cores had tie wraps around them and have hardened or broken off, replace them.

Battery Connections

Clean and or replace the battery connections if corrosion has eaten away at the connection or the cable.

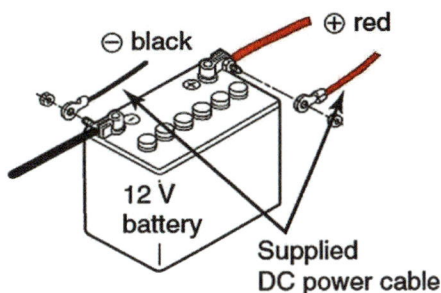

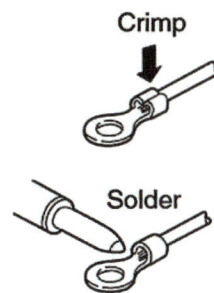

⊖ black   ⊕ red   Crimp

12 V battery

Supplied DC power cable

Solder

** Ham Band Stuff **

Appendix I
Made Simple for Cruisers Radio HF SSB Info

Example of West Coast Nets for North America
The schedule changes so go to Made Simple for Cruisers for the West Coast and download the latest information. This is a spreadsheet so the information may be easily updated by a cruiser.

Zulu Winter/Summer	Local Time Difference** 5:00	Name	Frequency USB/LSB Alternate Freqency	Coverage	Comments	WEB Site Updated 12SEP2012
~ 24 X 7		14.300 Nets	14.300 USB	East/West/South	Interncontinental / Maritime Mobile / Pacific Seafarers	http://14300.net
11:00 / 12:00	6:00 / 7:00	Intercon	14.300 USB	Carib & Pacific	From 07:00 - 12:00 ET	http://interconnet.org/
13:30	8:30	Picante	6.212 USB	Mexico	Net controls Puerto Vallarta.	N/A
14:00	9:00	Pan Pacific	8.143 USB 8.137 USB 8.155 USB	Central America	Pacific: South Pacific to Panama, Ecuador & the Galapagos and occasionally out to South Pacific.	N/A
14:00	9:00	Amigo	8.122 USB 8.116 USB 8.119 USB	Mexico	Mexico and Puddle Jumpers	N/A
14:30	9:30	Amigo	4.149 USB	Mexico	Approximate Time for Short-range net	N/A
14:30 / 13:30	9:30 / 8:30	Sonrisa	3.968 LSB	Mexico	Weather at UTC 13:45 Summer & 14:45 Winter.	http://sonrisanet.org/
15:30	10:30	Chubasco	7.192 LSB	Mexico	Warmup.	N/A
15:00 / 16:00	10:00 / 11:00	Baja California	7.2335 LSB	Mexico	Weather 15:15 / 16:15.	N/A
16:00	11:00	USCG Amature	14.300 USB		Saturday Only	http://www.w5cgc.org/
17:00 / 16:00	12:00 / 11:00	Maritime Mobile Service	14.300 USB	Carib & Pacific	From 17:00 - 03:0, Rene (K4EDX)	http://www.mmsn.org/
17:00	12:00	USCG Amature	14.327 USB		Saturday Only	http://www.w5cgc.org/
18:00	13:00	Manana	14.340 USB	Mexico	Monday-Saturday	http://reocities.com/TheTropics/3989/
21:00	16:00	Pacific Maritiime	21.402 USB	Pacific		http://pmmsn.net/
0:00	19:00	Happy Hour	3.968 LSB	Mexico		N/A
0:55	19:55	Southbound	8.122 USB	Mexico	Coverage area: Mexico	http://groups.yahoo.com/group/southbound_group
3:00	22:00	Pacific Seafarers	14.300 USB	South Pacific	Warmup 03:00 and roll-call 3:25 for underway vessels	http://www.pacseanet.com/

Made Simple for Cruisers

** Enter offset from UTC as a positive value, e.g. -7 hours is entered as "7:00".

		Marina SSB		
Summer		Amature SSB	Winter	

www.madesimpleforcruisers.com

Appendix II - Approximate Range of HF SSB signals

MHZ	APPROX RANGE		Ground Wave
	Sky Waves		
2 MHz	100 miles day	1000 miles night	150 miles
4 MHz	100 miles day	1500 miles night	100 miles
6 MHz	500 miles day	1500 miles night	75 miles
8 MHz	700 miles day	2000 miles night	70 miles
12 & 13 MHz	100 miles evenings	3000 miles days	50 miles
17 & 17 MHz	Unreliable evenings	4000 miles days	50 miles
22 MHz	Daytime only band	worldwide	~50 miles

Again this is only a guide and not a law of propagation.

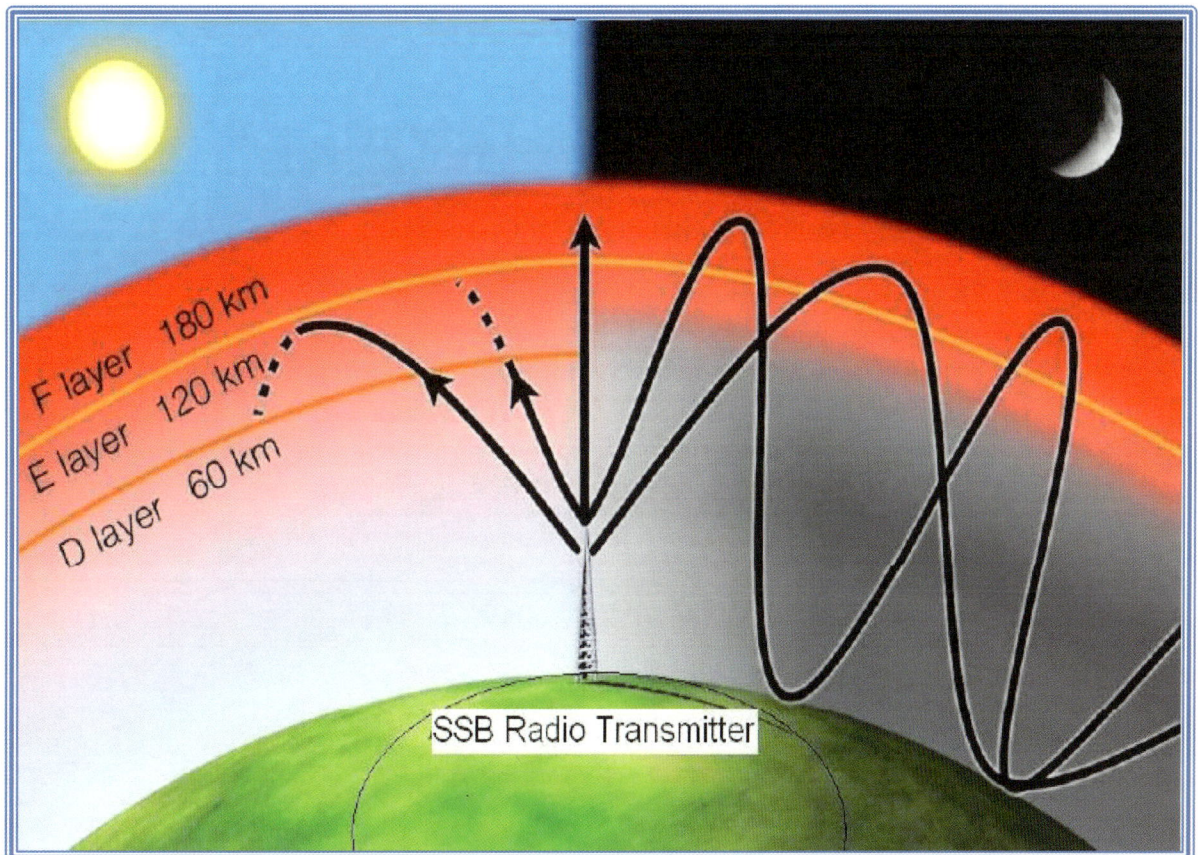

Appendix III - Ham Frequencies You May Use

US Ham Frequency Assignments

For the United States, the following frequencies are authorized for use by the respective class of license.

Technician:
- **80 Meters** 3.525-3.600 MHz: CW Only
- **40 Meters** 7.025-7.125 MHz : CW only
- **15 Meters** 21.025-21.200 MHz: CW Only
- **10 Meters** 28.000-28.300 MHz: CW, RTTY/Data--Maximum power 200 watts PEP
  28.300-28.500 MHz: CW, Phone--Maximum power 200 watts PEP
- **6 Meter** 50.0-50.1 MHz: CW Only
  50.1-54.0 MHz: CW, Phone, Image, MCW, RTTY/Data
- **70 Centimeters** 420.0-450.0 MHz: CW, Phone, Image, MCW, RTTY/Data

General:
- **160 Meters** 1.800-2.000 MHz: CW, Phone, Image, RTTY/Data
- **80 Meters** 3.525-3.600 MHz: CW, RTTY/Data
  3.800-4.000 MHz: CW, Phone, Image
- **40 Meters** 7.025-7.125 MHz : CW, RTTY/Data
  7.175-7.300 MHz:: CW, Phone, Image
- **30 Meters** 10.100-10.150 MHz: CW, RTTY/Data
- **20 Meters** 14.025 -14.150 MHz CW, RTTY/Data
  14.175 -14.350 MHz: CW, Phone, Image
- **17 Meters** 18.068-18.110 MHz: CW, RTTY/Data
  18.110-18.168 MHz: CW, Phone, Image
- **15 Meters** 21.025-21.200 MHz: CW, RTTY/Data
  21.275-21.450 MHz: CW, Phone, Image
- **12 Meters** 24.890-24.930 MHz: CW, RTTY/Data
  24.930-24.990 MHz: CW, Phone, Image
- **10 Meters** 28.000-28.300 MHz: CW, RTTY/Data
  28.300-29.700 MHz: CW, Phone, Image
- **6 Meter** 50.0-50.1 MHz: CW Only
  50.1-54.0 MHz: CW, Phone, Image, MCW, RTTY/Data
- **70 Centimeters** 420.0-450.0 MHz: CW, Phone, Image, MCW, RTTY/Data

Amateur Extra:

- **160 Meters** 1.800-2.000 MHz: CW, Phone, Image, RTTY/Data
- **80 Meters** 3.500-3.600 MHz: CW, RTTY/Data
  3.600-4.000 MHz: CW, Phone, Image
- **60 Meter** Selected Frequencies
- **40 Meters** 7.000-7.125 MHz : CW, RTTY/Data
  7.125-7.300 MHz:: CW, Phone, Image
- **30 Meters** 10.100-10.150 MHz: CW, RTTY/Data
- **20 Meters** 14.000 - 14.150 MHz CW, RTTY/Data
  14.150 -14.350 MHz: CW, Phone, Image
- **17 Meters** 18.068-18.110 MHz: CW, RTTY/Data
  18.110-18.168 MHz: CW, Phone, Image
- **15 Meters** 21.000-21.200 MHz: CW, RTTY/Data
  21.200-21.450 MHz: CW, Phone, Image
- **12 Meters** 24.890-24.930 MHz: CW, RTTY/Data
  24.930-24.990 MHz: CW, Phone, Image
- **10 Meters** 28.000-28.300 MHz: CW, RTTY/Data
  28.300-29.700 MHz: CW, Phone, Image
- **6 Meter** 50.0-50.1 MHz: CW Only
  50.1-54.0 MHz: CW, Phone, Image, MCW, RTTY/Data
- **2 Meters** 144.0-144.1 MHz: CW Only
  144.1-148.0 MHz: CW, Phone, Image, MCW, RTTY/Data
- **70 Centimeters** 420.0-450.0 MHz: CW, Phone, Image, MCW, RTTY/Data

There are also some really high frequencies that may be used by all Hams.

A good chart to have on board your boat to simplify determining where you can and cannot transmit is available from the American Radio Relay League (ARRL). The chart may be found at:

http://www.arrl.org/files/file/Hambands_color.pdf

Canadian HF Assigned Ham Frequency

Frequency (MHz) Lower edge	Frequency (MHz) Upper edge	Maximum Bandwidth	Qualifications
1.8	2.0	6 kHz	B+, B5 or BA
3.5	4.0	6 kHz	B+, B5 or BA
7.0	7.3	6 kHz	B+, B5 or BA
10.1	10.15	1 kHz	B+, B5 or BA
14.0	14.350	6 kHz	B+, B5 or BA
18.068	18.168	6 kHz	B+, B5 or BA
21.0	21.450	6 kHz	B+, B5 or BA
24.890	24.990	6 kHz	B+, B5 or BA
28.0	29.7	20 kHz	B+, B5 or BA

Notes:

"B" means an Amateur Operators Certificate with Basic Qualification, not authorized for HF SSB Frequency use.

"B+" means an Amateur Operators Certificate with Basic Qualification "with Honours" (where the holder achieved 80% or higher on the examination

"B5" means an Amateur Operators Certificate with Basic Qualification and Morse Code (5 w.p.m.) Qualification

"BA" means an Amateur Operators Certificate with Basic and Advanced Qualification

Appendix IV - NATO Phonetic Alphabet

Have this handy with your vessel and call signs to ensure good communications.

CHARACTER	MORSE CODE	TELEPHONY	PHONIC (PRONUNCIATION)
A	• —	Alfa	(AL-FAH)
B	— • • •	Bravo	(BRAH-VOH)
C	— • — •	Charlie	(CHAR-LEE) or (SHAR-LEE)
D	— • •	Delta	(DELL-TAH)
E	•	Echo	(ECK-OH)
F	• • — •	Foxtrot	(FOKS-TROT)
G	— — •	Golf	(GOLF)
H	• • • •	Hotel	(HOH-TEL)
I	• •	India	(IN-DEE-AH)
J	• — — —	Juliet	(JEW-LEE-ETT)
K	— • —	Kilo	(KEY-LOH)
L	• — • •	Lima	(LEE-MAH)
M	— —	Mike	(MIKE)
N	— •	November	(NO-VEM-BER)
O	— — —	Oscar	(OSS-CAH)
P	• — — •	Papa	(PAH-PAH)
Q	— — • —	Quebec	(KEH-BECK)
R	• — •	Romeo	(ROW-ME-OH)
S	• • •	Sierra	(SEE-AIR-RAH)
T	—	Tango	(TANG-GO)
U	• • —	Uniform	(YOU-NEE-FORM) or (OO-NEE-FORM)
V	• • • —	Victor	(VIK-TAH)
W	• — —	Whiskey	(WISS-KEY)
X	— • • —	Xray	(ECKS-RAY)
Y	— • — —	Yankee	(YANG-KEY)
Z	— — • •	Zulu	(ZOO-LOO)
1	• — — — —	One	(WUN)
2	• • — — —	Two	(TOO)
3	• • • — —	Three	(TREE)
4	• • • • —	Four	(FOW-ER)
5	• • • • •	Five	(FIFE)
6	— • • • •	Six	(SIX)
7	— — • • •	Seven	(SEV-EN)
8	— — — • •	Eight	(AIT)
9	— — — — •	Nine	(NIN-ER)
0	— — — — —	Zero	(ZEE-RO)

Sunnyside

Sierra
Uniform
November
November
Yankee
Sierra
India
Delta
Echo

AD7XL

Alpha, Delta, 7, Xray, Lima

WDA 5497

Whiskey, Delta Alpha 5497

NATO phonetic alphabet

90

Appendix V – Installing HF SSB?

Hints to Buying and Installing Your Marine HF SSB

It is recommended that when you purchase your marine radio, you obtain a complete package that includes all or at least the majority of the parts required for a successful installation.   You should also save money on the system by requesting all dealers bid exactly the same package.

Many cruisers purchase a marine radio and try and put the pieces together. If you have a good communications background, this may work for you, but it may cost you more for the system purchasing piece by piece.

If you plan to purchase an Icom IC M802 radio and plan to install the radio yourself, consider also purchasing my book, **"Icom IC M802 Starting from Scratch"**. The book includes discount coupons and should save you significantly in the purchase and proper installation of the radio. (Significantly more savings than the cost of the book!)

If you are not comfortable installing the system and decide to have a professional installer or a technical friend help, make sure they have experience installing marine HF SSB radios.

Contracting an Installation of a new Icom IC M802?
If you are not comfortable installing the radio yourself contract a local installer. However, make sure the installer is qualified and has installed marine radios before.
1. Contract a Commercial communications (FCC) licensed installer.
   a. While anyone may install the radio, a non-licensed installer may not legally test the transmitter functions of the radio.
2. Purchase a SWR meter and test the system yourself after the installer has completed and before you start transmitting.

** Marine Band Stuff **

Appendix VI - HF Marine Operators (WLO Radio)

WLO Radio has taken over all US HF based Marine Operators and is available on many frequencies. To sign up with them call 334-665-5110. Give them a credit card number to keep on file so that if in an emergency you need to make a call you do not have to broadcast your credit card number around the world.   They have had my card on file for years and will not charge you for anything but calls made.

WLO ITU CHANNELS

Channel Number	RX Frequency	TX Frequency
405	4369.0	4077.0
414	4396.0	4104.0
419	4411.0	4119.0
607	6519.0	6218.0
824	8788.0	8264.0
829	8803.0	8279.0
830	8806.0	8282.0
1212	13110.0	12263.0
1225	13149.0	12302.0
1226	13152.0	12305.0
1607	17260.0	16378.0
1641	17362.0	16480.0
1647	17380.0	16498.0
2237	22804.0	22108.0

KLB ITU CHANNELS - (KLB radio in the Pacific Northwest and Alaska)

Channel Number	RX Frequency	TX Frequency
417	4113.0	4405.0
608	6266.5	6318.0
805	8207.0	8731.0
1223	12488.0	12590.5

Contact Rene Stiegler of WLO/KLB radio for information and frequency information packs.
PH: (334)665-5110, FX:(334)666-8339, or wloemail@aol.com or rene@shipcom.com

Appendix VII - Understanding MMSI Numbers

The first digit of an MMSI

The meaning of the first digit is: 0 Ship group, coast station, or group of coast stations; 1 Assigned for use by SAR aircraft; 2-7 MMSI's used by individual ships, beginning with an MID below.

- **2 Europe**
- **3 North and Central America and Caribbean**
- **4 Asia**
- **5 Oceana**
- **6 Africa**
- **7 South America**
- **8 Assigned for regional Use**
- **9 Recently re-assigned to Nav aids and also craft associated with a parent ship (ITU-R recommendation M.585-4)**

Maritime identification digits (MID)

MIDXXXXXX - A MID consists of 3 digits, always starting with a digit from 2 to 7. It is a 9-digit code to constitute a ship station identity.

Group ship station call identities

Group ship station call identities for calling simultaneously more than one ship are formed as follows: **0MIDXXXXX - T**he first figure is zero and X is any figure from 0 to 9. The particular MID represents only the country assigning the group ship station call identity and so does not prevent group calls to fleets containing more than one ship nationality.

Coast station identities

Coast station identities are formed as follows: **00MIDXXXX** - The first two figures are zeros and X is any figure from 0 to 9. The MID reflects the country in which the coast station or coast earth station is located.

Group coast station call identities

Group coast station call identities for calling simultaneously more than one coast station are formed as a subset of coast station identities, as follows: **00MIDXXXX - T**he first two figures are zeros and X is any figure from 0 to 9.

In the United States
In the U.S., federal MMSIs are assigned by the National Telecommunications and Information Administration, and are normally, but not always, formed as 3669XXXXX.

Non-federal MMSI numbers are assigned by the FCC normally as part of the ship station license application, and are formed as 366XXX000 for ships on international voyages and ships needing an Inmarsat mobile earth station, or 366XXXXX0 for all other ships.

The United States Coast Guard group

Ship station call identity is 036699999

Group Coast station call identity is 003669999.

Appendix VIII - MMSI Numbers
For US Coast Guard Stations

Astoria	Oregon	003669935
Boston	Massachusetts	003669927
Boston	Massachusetts	003669991
Brant Point	Massachusetts	003669902
Cape Arago	Oregon	003669911
Cape Hatteras	North Carolina	003669906
Cape Hinchinbrook	Alaska	003669924
Cape May	New Jersey	003669903
Cape Yakataga	Alaska	003669924
Charleston	South Carolina	003669907
Chincoteague	Virginia	003669932
Chokoloski	Florida	003669917
Corpus Christi	Texas	003669916
Fort Macon	North Carolina	003669920
Freeport	Texas	003669915
Ft. Pierce	Florida	003669919
Ft. Stephens	Oregon	003669935
Galveston	Texas	003669915
Grande Isle	Louisiana	003669908
Hampton Roads	Virginia	003669933
Honolulu	Hawaii	003669905
Humboldt Bay	California	003669909
Islamorada	Florida	003669919
Jumeau	Alaska	003669922
Ketchikan	Alaska	003669923
Key West	Florida	003669918
Kodiak	Alaska	003669899
Lena Point	Alaska	003669922
Long Beach	California	003669912
Lualuaei	Hawaii	003669905
Marathon	Florida	003669918
Mayport	Florida	003669925
Miami	Florida	003669997

Miami	Florida	003669919
Mobile	Alabama	003669914
Monterey	California	003669910
Moriches	New York	003669936
Mullet Key	Florida	003669917
New Haven	Connecticut	003669931
New Orleans	Louisiana	003669998
New Orleans	Louisiana	003669908
New York	New York	003669930
North Bend	Oregon	003669911
Point Arena	California	003669909
Point Conception	California	003669912
Point Pinos	California	003669910
Port Angeles	Washington	003669904
Port Isabel	Texas	003669916
Portland	Oregon	003669934
Porstmouth	Virginia	003669995
Point Higgins	Alaska	003669923
Quillayute	Washington	003669904
Saint Petersburg	Florida	003669917
San Clemente	California	003669913
San Diego	California	003669913
Sandy Hook	New Jersey	003669929
San Francisco	California	003669926
San Francisco - Pt. Reyes	California	003669990
San Juan	Puerto Rico	003669992
Santa Rosa	California	003669914
Shinnecock	New York	003669936
South Portland	Maine	003669928
Southwest Harbor	Maine	003669921
Sullivan s Island	South Carolina	003669907
Valdez	Alaska	003669924
Venice	Florida	003669917
Woods Hole	Massachusetts	003669902
Yakutat	Alaska	003669922

For Canada Coast Guard Stations

Comox	British Columbia	003160014
Halifax	Nova Scotia	003160016
Inuvik	Northwest Territory	003160024
Iqaluit	Nunavut	003160023
Labrador	Labrador	003160022
Les Escoumins	Quebec	003160026
Montreal	Quebec	003160028
Placentia	Newfoundland	003160019
Port aux Basques	Newfoundland	003160018
Prescott	Ontario	003160029
Prince Rupert	British Columbia	003160013
Quebec	Quebec	003160027
Riviere-au-Renard	Quebec	003160025
St. Anthony	Newfoundland	003160021
Saint John	New Brunswick	003160015
St. John's	Newfoundland	003160020
Samia	Ontario	003160030
Sydney	Nova Scotia	003160017
Thunder Bay	Ontario	003160031
Tofino	British Columbia	003160012
Vancouver	British Columbia	003160010
Victoria	British Columbia	003160011

Appendix VIX - Establishing Group MMSI IDs

The key for a group MMSI number is that they should be unique to minimize the group size and the first digit will always be a zero. Two zeros are used for shore stations.

USA individual MMSI assigned by the FCC will end in a zero. To create a group identity, take any one of the group member's individual MMSI numbers, move the zero at the end of the number to the beginning. That new number should be unique and will be your new group identity.

For example, if your individual identity is 366123450, you would create a group ID as 036612345. However, even 012345678 will work fine.

If your country's MMSI numbers do not end with a 0, shift the number right anyway and insert a zero as the leading number. That number should also be a unique number.

All vessels participating in the group need to have the Group MMSI number programmed into their radios.

If by chance the number is not unique, the worst thing that can happen is another group might join in with your group. The chances are very low that this will occur using the process above.

Appendix VX - Important Frequencies

Coast Guard HF SSB – Distress and Initial Contact

Stations authorized for the handling of Distress message traffic and initial contact with United States Coast Guard Long Range Communication facilities.

KHz SHIP STATION	KHz COAST STATION	NMF	NMN	NMA	NMG
4125	4125	2300-1100Z	2300-1100Z	2300-1100Z	2300-1100Z
6215	6215	24 HRS	24 HRS	24 HRS	24 HRS
8291	8291	24 HRS	24 HRS	24 HRS	24 HRS
12290	12290	1100-2300Z	1100-2300Z	1100-2300Z	1100-2300Z

KHz SHIP STATION	KHz COAST STATION	Station and Schedule (UTC)		
		NMC	NMO	NOJ
4125	4125	24 HRS	0600-1800Z	24 HRS
6215	6215	24 HRS	24 HRS	24 HRS
8291	8291	24 HRS	24 HRS	
12290	12290	24 HRS	1800-0600Z	

Distress and Emergency Working Channels		
Working Channel	RX	TX
4 MHz	4,426.0 KHz	4,134.0 KHz
6 MHz	6,501.0 KHz	6,200.0 KHz
8 MHz	8,764.0 KHz	8,240.0 KHz
12 MHz	13,089.0 KHz	12,242.0 KHz
16 MHz	17,314.0 KHz	16,432.0 KHz

HF SSB Distress Channels for Digital Selective Calling

These channels are scanned and monitored by DSC capable radio's built in emergency receiver that is connected to the DERA.

Portsmouth/NMN, Boston/NMF, Miami/NMA, New Orleans/NMG, Pt. Reyes/NMC, Honolulu HI/NMO, Kodiak AK/NOJ	
2187.5 kHz	Coast Guard will normally respond to DSC test calls if acknowledgment is requested. Reports of un-cancelled or unacknowledged inadvertently transmitted distress calls will be forwarded to the Federal Communications Commission.
4207.5 kHz	
6312.0 kHz	
8414.5 kHz	
12577.0 kHz	
16804.5 kHz	

7X24 Telephone Numbers - Help with Missing Vessels

For help with missing vessels outside the United States waters.

District 1	Boston, MA	617-223-8443	
District 5	Portsmouth, VA	757-398-6390	
District 7	Miami, FL	305-415-6820	
District 8	New Orleans	504-671-2230	
District 11	Alameda, CA	510-437-3701	Email: rccalameda1@uscg.mil
District 13	Seattle, WA	800-982-8813	
District 14	Honolulu, HI	800-818-8724	
District 17	Juneau, AK	907-463-2242	

Appendix XI - What to do When Receiving a Distress Call

Actions of Cruiser in receipt of a distress alert

Cruisers receiving a DSC distress alert from another vessel should normally not acknowledge the alert by DSC since acknowledgement of a DSC distress alert by use of DSC is normally made by coast stations only.

Only if no other station seems to have received the DSC distress alert, and the transmission of the DSC distress alert continues, the cruiser should acknowledge the DSC distress alert by use of DSC to terminate the call. The cruiser should then inform a coast station or a coast earth station by any practicable means.

Cruisers receiving a DSC distress alert from another vessel should also defer the acknowledgement of the distress alert by radiotelephony for a short interval, if the other vessel is within an area covered by one or more coast stations, in order to give the coast station time to acknowledge the DSC distress alert first.

Cruisers receiving a DSC distress alert from another vessel shall:
Watch for the reception of a distress acknowledgement on the distress channel (2187.5 kHz on MF/HF and channel 70 on VHF):

1. Prepare for receiving the subsequent distress communication by tuning the radio receiver to the distress traffic frequency in the same band in which the DSC distress alert was received i.e. 2182 kHz on MF, channel 16 on VHF.
2. Acknowledge the receipt of the distress alert by transmitting the following by radio on the distress traffic frequency in the same band in which the DSC distress alert was received, i.e. 2182 kHz on MF, channel 16 on VHF:

"MAYDAY", the 9-digit identity of the vessel in distress, repeated 3 times, "this is", the 9-digit identity or the call sign or other identification of own vessel, repeated 3 times, "RECEIVED MAYDAY".

e.g. "Mayday sailing vessel Sunshine, Mayday sailing vessel Sunshine, Mayday sailing vessel Sunshine, this is the sailing vessel Eagle I have received your Mayday, this is the sailing vessel Eagle I have received your Mayday, this is the sailing vessel Eagle, I have received your Mayday"

NOTE - Vessels out of range of a distress event or not able to assist should only acknowledge if no other station appears to acknowledge the receipt of the DSC distress alert.

See the flow chart below for an overview of the process. The entire procedure is posted and downloadable on my website on the Icom page.

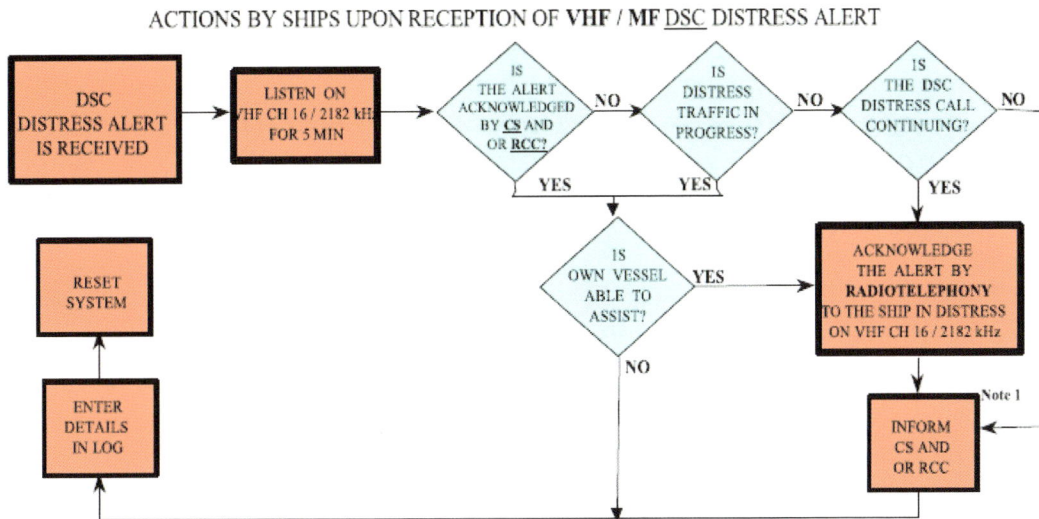

ACTIONS BY SHIPS UPON RECEPTION OF **VHF / MF** <u>DSC</u> DISTRESS ALERT

```
┌──────────────┐     ┌──────────────┐        ◇ IS THE ALERT           ◇ IS DISTRESS         ◇ IS THE DSC
│     DSC      │     │  LISTEN ON   │          ACKNOWLEDGED   NO        TRAFFIC IN    NO      DISTRESS CALL   NO
│ DISTRESS ALERT│───▶│VHF CH 16/2182 kHz│──▶   BY CS AND    ───▶       PROGRESS?    ───▶     CONTINUING?    ───▶
│ IS RECEIVED  │     │  FOR 5 MIN   │          OR RCC?                                                         │
└──────────────┘     └──────────────┘            YES                     YES                    YES           │
```

DSC DISTRESS ALERT IS RECEIVED

LISTEN ON VHF CH 16 / 2182 kH FOR 5 MIN

IS THE ALERT ACKNOWLEDGED BY CS AND OR RCC? NO

IS DISTRESS TRAFFIC IN PROGRESS? NO

IS THE DSC DISTRESS CALL CONTINUING? NO

YES   YES   YES

IS OWN VESSEL ABLE TO ASSIST? YES

NO

ACKNOWLEDGE THE ALERT BY **RADIOTELEPHONY** TO THE SHIP IN DISTRESS ON VHF CH 16 / 2182 kHz

Note 1

RESET SYSTEM

ENTER DETAILS IN LOG

INFORM CS AND OR RCC

REMARKS:

Note 1 :   Appropriate or relevant RCC and/or Coast Station shall be informed accordingly. If further DSC alerts are received from the same source and the ship in distress is beyond doubt in the vicinity, a DSC acknowledgement may, after consultation with an RCC or Coast Station, be sent to terminate the call.

Note 2 :   In no case is a ship permitted to transmit a DSC distress delay call on receipt of a DSC distress alert on either VHF or MF channels.

CS = Coast Station   RCC = Rescue Co-ordination Center

***

102

Appendix XII - Who Else is on HF Radio

For the latest schedule of English broadcasts around the world go to Prime Time Shortwave at: http://www.primetimeshortwave.com

Example of HF Broadcasts

Country	Call Sign	Time	When	Frequency
Canada	CBCNQ	0000-0100	NA	9625
Canada	CFRX	0000-2400	NA	6070
Canada	CFVP	0000-		6030
Canada	CKZN	0000-2400	NA	6160
Canada	CKZU	0000-2400	NA	6160
Canada	R. Canada Int'l	1800-1859	Af	9740ch, 11845va, 15365, 17790
U. S. A.	AFRTS	0000-2400	NA	5446.5 USB, 7811 USB, 12133.5 USB
U. S. A.	Disco Palace	2000-2100	NA	17755fg drm
U. S. A.	KJES	1900-2000	Oc	15385
U. S. A.	Pan American	1930-2030	ME, Af, Sa	6040ge
U. S. A.	V. of America	0000-0030	ME	7560ku
U. S. A.	WBCQ	2200-2400	Am, F-Tu	7415
U. S. A.	WEWN	0000-0600	ME	11520
U. S. A.	WHRI	0300-0500	NA, Tu-Sa	7315
U. S. A.	WJHR	1400-2200	NA	15550
U. S. A.	Wld Univ Net	1300-2400	NA	13845
U. S. A.	WRMI	0000-1500	LA	9955
U. S. A.	WRNO	0200-0500	NA	7505
U. S. A.	WTJC	0000-2400	NA	9370
U. S. A.	WTWW	0000-1200	NA,Eu,Af	5755

Appendix XIII - Marine HF Ship to Ship Frequencies

ID	2 MHz	4 MHz	6 MHz	8 MHz	12 MHz
A	2065.0 kHz	4146 kHz	6224 kHz	8294 kHz	12353 kHz
B	2079.0 kHz	4149 kHz	6227 kHz	8297 kHz	12356 kHz
C	2093.0 kHz		6230 kHz		12359 kHz
D	2096.5 kHz				12362 kHz
E	2214.0 kHz				12365 kHz
F					
G					

ID	16 MHz	18 MHz	22 MHz	25 MHz
A	16528 kHz	18825 kHz	22159 kHz	25100 kHz
B	16531 kHz	18828 kHz	22162 kHz	25103 kHz
C	16534 kHz	18831 kHz	22165 kHz	25106 kHz
D	16537 kHz	18834 kHz	22168 kHz	25109 kHz
E	16540 kHz	18837 kHz	22171 kHz	25112 kHz
F	16543 kHz	18840 kHz	22174 kHz	25115 kHz
G	16546 kHz	18843 kHz	22177 kHz	25118 kHz

Appendix XIV – ICOM IC M802 Overview

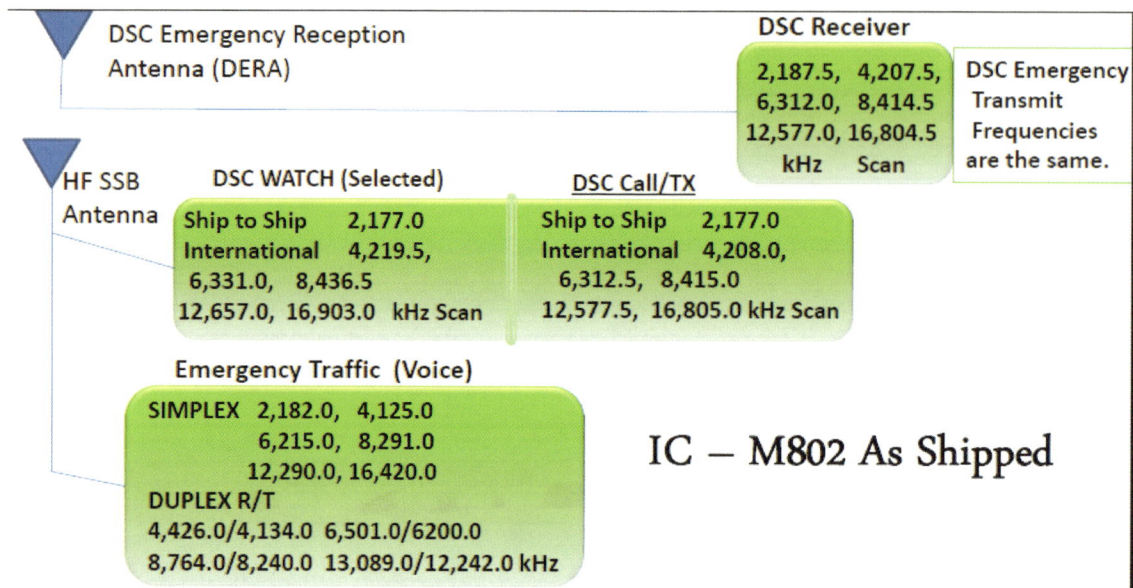

DSC Emergency Reception Antenna (DERA)

DSC Receiver

2,187.5, 4,207.5, 6,312.0, 8,414.5 12,577.0, 16,804.5 kHz Scan

DSC Emergency Transmit Frequencies are the same.

HF SSB Antenna

DSC WATCH (Selected)

Ship to Ship 2,177.0
International 4,219.5,
6,331.0, 8,436.5
12,657.0, 16,903.0 kHz Scan

DSC Call/TX

Ship to Ship 2,177.0
International 4,208.0,
6,312.5, 8,415.0
12,577.5, 16,805.0 kHz Scan

Emergency Traffic (Voice)

SIMPLEX 2,182.0, 4,125.0
6,215.0, 8,291.0
12,290.0, 16,420.0
DUPLEX R/T
4,426.0/4,134.0 6,501.0/6200.0
8,764.0/8,240.0 13,089.0/12,242.0 kHz

IC – M802 As Shipped

Programming information at: http://www.made-simplefor-cruisers.com/ic-m802-2

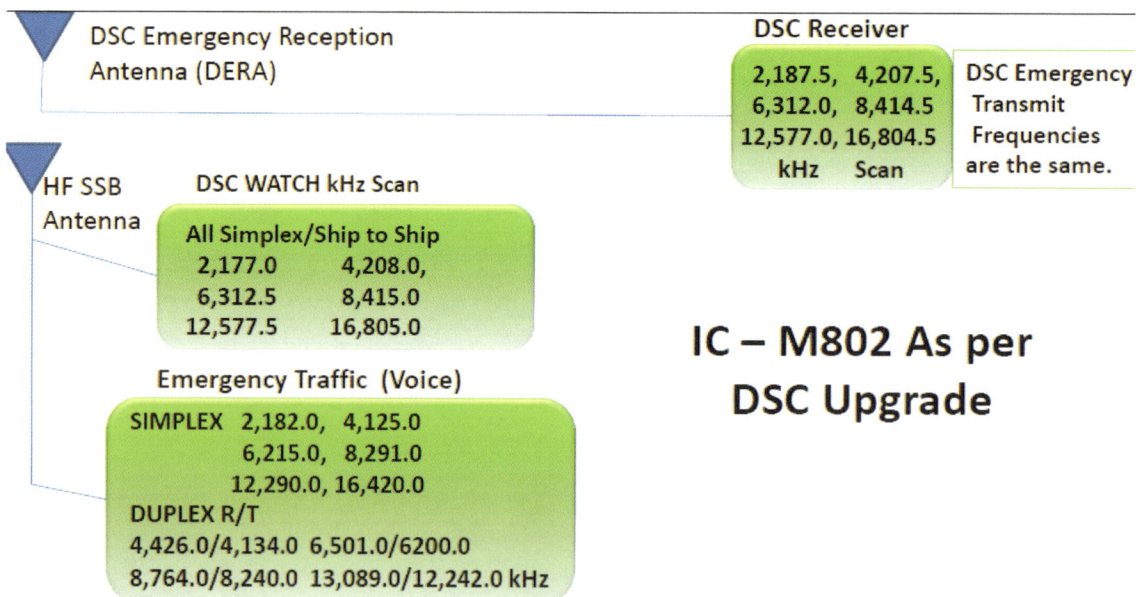

DSC Emergency Reception Antenna (DERA)

DSC Receiver

2,187.5, 4,207.5, 6,312.0, 8,414.5 12,577.0, 16,804.5 kHz Scan

DSC Emergency Transmit Frequencies are the same.

HF SSB Antenna

DSC WATCH kHz Scan

All Simplex/Ship to Ship
2,177.0 4,208.0,
6,312.5 8,415.0
12,577.5 16,805.0

Emergency Traffic (Voice)

SIMPLEX 2,182.0, 4,125.0
6,215.0, 8,291.0
12,290.0, 16,420.0
DUPLEX R/T
4,426.0/4,134.0 6,501.0/6200.0
8,764.0/8,240.0 13,089.0/12,242.0 kHz

IC – M802 As per DSC Upgrade

Appendix XV – Things that Cause Static

HF SSB radios are subject to amplitude type noise as discussed earlier in this book. The following are a list of typical sources for noise in your radio.

On the Boat

- Chargers
- Refrigerators
- Alternators
- Solar Regulators
- Water makers (Spectra has been noted as creating noise in the idle mode)
- Pumps
- Air Conditioning Systems
- Other Electronics on board

At an Anchorage

- Other Boats components as above

In a Marina

- Other Boats components as above
- Pumps from Swimming pools
- Large Yachts have an endless supply of noise makers that can creep into your HF SSB

Appendix XVI – Dialing in a Station

There are many different types of radios that cruisers tend to use. Keeping this in mind, it would take an entire new book to explain how to operate, tune and program the many types of radios. The following is a general guideline to follow.

1. Make sure the radio will receive signals
   a. Using the dial tune the radio to 10,000kHz, 15,000 kHz and 20,000 kHz. This frequency is station WWV the US time and frequency standard out of Fort Collins, CO. The station operates 24 hours per day and provides an exact UTC time mark each minute.
   b. At least one of these frequencies should come in loud and clear if you are in or near the US.
   c. If you are in the Pacific Ocean, there is also WWVH in Hawaii that transmits on 25,000 kHz.

2. Prepare the radio for Communications
   a. Consider programming the frequencies you plan to use into the radios user programming space. Marine radios have 160 available locations to store frequently used channels.
   b. You can program both Simplex and Duplex frequencies in each user channel.

3. Set the transceiver up to talk
   a. Select a frequency you plan to talk on from the programmed channels.
   b. If you have an automatic tuner, press the tune button.
   c. If you do not have an automatic tuner, you should have a power and SWR meter attached to your transceiver output. While watching the meter, key the microphone and whistle or make aloud "Day OOOOO" sound into the microphone until the SWR is low.

4. Begin talking
   a. Be sure and use the Name of vessel and Call Sign as appropriate.

5. Example
   a. Caller: Sailing Vessel Rain Dancer this is the sailing Vessel Sunnyside, Alpha Delta 7 X-Ray Lima.
   b. Receiver: This is the Sailing Vessel Rain Dancer Alpha Bravo 6 X-Ray Lima.
   c. Caller: Hi Dan ………….
   d. Etc
   e. Caller: This is Alpha Delta 7 X-Ray Lima and I am clear.
   f. Receiver: Alpha Bravo 6 X-Ray Lima clear.

KISS Dictionary

Airmail – PC Software used for both Sailmail and Winlink email systems. The Sailmail and Winlink versions are slightly different, but may run together on the same computer. The Airmail program was written by Jim Corenman.

Amateur HF Band Frequencies – The FCC has allocated specific frequencies within the HF band to radio amateur. To transmit on these frequencies you must pass exams for Technician and General Class Amateur. It is illegal in all countries to transmit on these channels as they are also controlled internationally by the ITU. (Except in an emergency)

The frequencies within the Amateur radio:

1.8MHZ to 2MHz (MHF band)	160 Meter Band – LSB
3.5MHZ to 4MHz	80 Meter Band – LSB
5.3305MHz to 5.4035MHz – 50 watts maximum	60 Meter Band – USB
7MHz to7.3MHZ	40 Meter Band – LSB
10.1MHz to 10.15MHz	30 Meter Band – RTTY/Data
14MHz to 14.35MHz	20 Meter Band – USB
18.068MHz to 18.168MHz	17 Meter Band – USB
21.025MHz to 21.45MHz	15 Meter Band – USB
24.89MHz to 24.99MHz	12 Meter Band – USB
28MHz to 29.7MHz	10 Meter Band – USB

Amateur Packet Radio – Communications over Amateur radio between two computers.

Amplitude – The level of voltage or current for audio or radio frequencies.

Amplitude Modulation – "AM" contains a carrier frequency (the one you tune to receive the signal) and "intelligence" in the Upper Sideband, Lower Sidebands.

Ampere – Unit used to measure current flow and uses the symbol I. I = Voltage/Resistance

AF – Audio Frequency. The Audio frequency band is 20Hz to 20,000Hz, but most of us old guys only make it to about 10-12,000Hz. Most dogs hear the 20,000Hz fine.

Analog – Continuous voltage levels that may change gradually or rapidly as opposed to digital that changes from a one to a zero and back near instantaneously. An analog reading of a voltage tells us what the voltage is. Depending on the resolution it take 8, 16, or, 32 bits in digital to define the analog voltage measured.

Antenna – A device or structure used to receive to transmit electromagnetic waves.

Band – A group of frequencies. Similar to the AM band and FM band the HF Band includes all the frequencies from 3MHz to 30MHz.

Bandwidth – The frequencies that are allowed to come into the radio above and below the radio's tuned frequency. If the radio is tuned at 1,000kHz, but it will allow 9980kHz up to 1,020kHz the radio would have a 40kHz Bandwidth.

Baud – Baud is the number of bits per second transmitted.

Baud Rate – Baud rate is the measure of for serial communications such as with a modem.

Bits per second bps – BPS is the rate at which bits stream in a serial communication. 300 bps is also 300 baud. If a word is 10 bits, then 300 baud would be 30 characters per second or 30cps.

Bonding –Tying together all major metal items on a boat that extend into the water to control/reduce galvanic corrosion on a boat.

Call Frequency – Are the transmit and receive frequencies that will be used for digital data such as Latitude, longitude, time, MMSI number etc. sent as a Digital Selective Calling (DSC) message or acknowledgements to a DSC message sent by another vessel.

Carrier Signal – Base frequency to which the modulation or intelligence is applied in order to be transmitted. The carrier signal may be modulated using Frequency modulation (FM), Amplitude modulation (AM) or several other forms of applying intelligence to a radio transmittable frequency.

Clarity – Clarity is typically used on Single Sideband radios to adjust the received frequency for better understandability of an incoming signal while the transmitter signal remains on the assigned frequency. Some older radios, may not be transmitting on the exact frequency and as a result the Donald Duck effect from being off frequency may make it hard to understand the other station.

Coaxial Cable – Special cable used to connect two radio frequency devices that contain a center conductor and a mesh cable that completely surrounds the center conductor. Examples: RG8U, RG213, RG58 for Communications and RG59 for TV cable.

CW – Continuous Wave. CW is typically used by Amateur radio operators and others. The carrier frequency, the frequency tuned to on the radio, is turned off and on at a rate representing Morris code. The intelligence is then the carrier turning on and off.

Cycles Per Second – CPS was re-named to Hertz (Hz) many years ago as folks frequently took a short cut and just called it cycles which does not give a time reference. Hz is always CPS.

Counterpoise – Ground side of an antenna system made out of copper strip or mesh. Also referred to as ground plane.

DERA – *This is the* "DSC Emergency Reception Antenna". As Named by this Author. DERA is a broad frequency range reception antenna that is connected to the antenna 2 position on the IC M802. Without this antenna no Distress calls, acknowledgments, urgent or ships calls will be heard.

DSC – Digital Selective Calling. A digital transmission used to contact other stations in emergencies or just to call a friend making connection without using a hailing channel.

DSC Receiver – A special purpose receiver built into the IC-M802 that monitors Distress frequency transmissions using J2B modulation (digital SSB).

Email Ready – Marine HF SSB that is capable of sending email. Email requires the transmitter be capable of full power for one or two minutes as the transmitter cycles between receive and transmit. Older analog HF SSB unit were not built to transmit full power for minutes at a time.

Emission – This is another way of saying how the intelligence is applied to the carrier frequency. Common emission types include AM and FM. With SSB, upper and lower sideband are frequently used. Emission types used by the IC – M802:

- *A1A (CW)* – Double-sideband amplitude modulation (e.g. AM broadcast radio); One channel containing digital information; Aural telegraphy, intended to be decoded by ear, such as Morse code.
- *F1B (FSK)* – FM broadcast radio; One channel containing digital information; Electronic telegraphy, intended to be decoded by machine.
- *H3E* – Single-sideband with full carrier; One channel containing analogue information; Voice or Music intended to be listened to by a human.
- *J2B (Receive Only)* – Single-sideband with suppressed carrier; One channel containing digital information, using a subcarrier; Electronic telegraphy, intended to be decoded by machine.
- *J3E (USB/LSB)* – Single-sideband with suppressed carrier; One channel containing analogue information; Voice or Music intended to be listened to by a human.
- *JB3* – Upper Sideband transmission

Frequency – The number of times a signal goes from zero volts to Max positive volts to zero volts to max negative to zero volts in a period of one second. Cycle per second measured in Hertz.

Frequency Modulation – (FM) is where a carrier frequency, the frequency you tune the radio to, and the carrier frequency changes with the "intelligence". When the transmitted frequency is equal to (and not changing) the carrier frequency, the radio is quiet, "No Intelligence".

Galvanic Corrosion – Corrosion that destroys metal as a result of current flowing between two metal objects usually in water. Two metal objects with saltwater between them forms a small battery. Shorting the two metal objects with wire eliminates any voltage difference and thus current flow.

Ground Wave – A radio signal that travels along the surface of the earth.

Hertz – unit of measure of frequency. One hertz = 1Hz = 1 complete cycle in one second.

HF Email – Email that is sent by your computer to a modem and then the radio. A subscription or Amateur Radio license is required for HF email.

Impedance – The opposition to the flow of current as a result of resistance capacitance and inductance within a circuit.

ITU – International Telecommunications Union based in Geneva, Switzerland. The ITU is the Czar for world communications. Countries input frequency needs and the ITU keeps us all from over running each other.

110

kHz – Kilo Hertz, is thousands of cycles per second

LSB Transmission – Lower Side Band Transmission. A form of Amplitude modulation where the carrier frequency and the Upper Sideband are eliminated to allow all the power in the radio to be output in the one upper sideband. No power is sent out except when "intelligence" is added through the microphone or modem.

Marine Frequencies Bands – Marine HF SSB bands. Some of the frequencies also include Amateur band, but again, the license is required. [Upper side band (USB) Only]

- 1.6MHz to 2.9999MHz
- 4.0MHz to 4.9999MHz
- 6.0 MHz to 6.9999MHz
- 8.0MHz to 8.9999MHz
- 12.0MHz to 13.9999MHz
- 16.0MHz to 17.9999MHz
- 18.0MHz to 19.9999MHz
- 22.0MHz to 22.9999MHz
- 25.0MHz to 27.5MHz

MHz – Mega Hertz, is millions of cycles per second

Modem – A device connected between your computer and the HF radio that changes the digital signals out of the computer to a signal that can be sent over the HF Band. Pactor modems seem to be the most popular for cruisers.

Morse Code – Morse Code is a method of communicating by turning the carrier frequency on and off or a modulating tone on and off at a specific rate for marks and spaces. Morse Code requires both the sender and receiver to know the code resulting in intelligence being transferred from one location to another.

NMEA – A signal format that is used to move information via wires from point "A" to point "B". Typical data would include GPS position and time data.

NEMA 0183 Version 3.01 – Is the NMEA connection on the IC M802 is for some reason a BNC coaxial connector instead of the standard two wire or terminal connections. While this may increase the difficulty of inputting the GPS signal, you can by factory made BNC cables that may be cut and used for this connection. The IC M802 requires sentence" **GGA**" to be sent to read the GPS.

Pactor – A frequency shift keying mode. Pactor format is used to modulate HF SSB radios using a Pactor modem to send emails.

Pactor Protocol Software – This is the software is used to compress/decompress and modulate/demodulate the transceiver. Pactor 3 protocol is 3 to 4 times faster than Pactor 2 and Pactor 4 is twice that of Pactor 3. The assumption here is that both the email service and the user are utilizing the same level of protocol. If you have a Pactor 4 protocol modem, the modem will also talk to Pactor stations with Pactor 2 and Pactor 3 protocol at the slowest modems in the links speed. Pactor 4 software is claimed to be twice as fast as Pactor 3 software. However this is only when talking to another Pactor 4 unit. The slowest Pactor in the link rules.

Pile Ups – More than one station trying to transmit at the same time and as a result no one is really understood. Usually just a lot of noise.

Propagation Tool – This software tool will help communicators determine what frequency has a chance of linking up with another location. The tool will tell you what will not work and only what might work as the tool only knows basic propagation information and not about cloud cover, local noise and storms that may impact actual communications.

RF Radio Frequency – Frequencies that are made up of electromagnetic energy and may be used to transmit intelligence. RF is generally thought of as high frequency, but there are also transmitters that broadcast in the audio frequency range. They are transmitting electromagnetic waves and not sound waves, so you cannot actually hear the transmission without a receiving device.

Received Signal – A small signal collected on the antenna that is amplified by the radio and turned back into information or intelligence.

R-S-T Signal Reporting – Readability by Signal Strength

Readability: 1 = unreadable, 2 =Barely readable, 3 = Readable with difficulty, 4 = No difficulty, 5 = Perfect.

Strength: 1=Faint,2=very week, 3=weak, 4=fair, 5=fairly good, 6=good, 7=moderately strong, 8 strong, 9= very strong   (E.g. "I read you 4 by 6" is readable with a good signal.)

Scan – An automated method of looking at many frequencies, one at a time, to help look for transmitting stations.

Sensitivity – This term applies to how well the receiver portion of the radio can convert the very small received signal into intelligence you can hear in the speaker.

SFI – Solar Flux Index, a factor that is used to help predict the best frequency to use by a Propagation tool.

Sky Wave – Radio signals that bounce to and from the Ionosphere and the earth's surface.

Snap on Ferrite Cores – These devices are used around cables to act as a block to RF into a device. Often computer equipment includes ferrite cores that are pre-molded onto the cable. Cruisers should consider putting ferrite cores on every cable connection for your radio, modem, and computer equipment as well as other devices around the boat that turn on or off when transmitting on HF SSB radio.

Speed of light and radio waves – 300,000,000Meters per second.

Spurious emissions – Unwanted frequencies and that are not within the designed bandwidth of the radio.

Single Side Band (SSB) – A transmission mode where the carrier frequency and one of the sidebands are suppressed such that the only energy radiated is contained in one sideband.   SSB can be Upper Sideband (USB) or Lower Sideband (LSB) transmission.

Traffic Frequency – Traffic frequencies are the transmitted and the received frequencies that will be used for voice communications.   Transmit and receive frequencies will be entered as the same frequency for simplex operation and different for duplex operation.

Transmitted Signal – Is the electromagnetic signal that propagates from the antenna. The radiated signal is created from a large power signal that is fed to the antenna where it creates the electromagnetic field around the antenna and then radiates the signal in to the atmosphere.

Tropospheric Propagation – Also called Tunneling. Tunneling allows signal refraction for frequencies above 30MHz such as VHF radio.   Result from atmospheric conditions such as temperature inversions.

Tuner – The box in between the radio output and the antenna that is responsible for matching the antenna to the transmitter to minimize SWR and maximize radiated power from the antenna.

USB Transmission – Upper Side Band Transmission.   A form of Amplitude modulation where the carrier frequency and the Lower Sideband are eliminated to allow all the power in the radio to be output in the one upper sideband.   No power is sent out except when "intelligence" is added through the microphone or modem.

Standing Wave Ratio (SWR) – SWR is not a good thing. The number represents the amount of power that is sent out of a transmitter to the antenna, but bounces back because of a poor antenna match.   High SWR can hurt your radio. The Antenna Tuner is responsible to keep the SWR low, but must have an adequate antenna and ground system to work effectively.   From forward power and reflected power you may calculate SWR.   Under the Communications page on www.made-simplefor-cruisers.com there is a spread sheet that will allow you to calculate and save SWR history.

Transceiver – A radio that is capable of both transmitting signal and receiving signal capability.

Tuner – An automated device that adjusts the electrical length of an antenna and grounding system to the proper length to match the requirements for the output of a transmitter.

USB – Upper Sideband is used to send intelligence and the lower sideband LSB and carrier are suppressed.

UTC – Universal Coordinated Time. UTC is essentially the same as Greenwich Mean Time. Coordinated Universal Time is a time standard based on an International Atomic Time. UTC is also referred to as Zulu time.

Winlink 2000 – Amateur radio sponsored and supported email service provider.
WL2K – Winlink 2000 is the connecting station for the Amateur email system.
Wave Length – Wave Length is the distance a complete cycle would extend as it is moving away from the source. In the case of the radio transmission it would be the distance the beginning of the cycle has moved, at approximately the speed of light, when the last part of the cycle leaves the transmitter.
Wave Length in meters is = 300/Frequency in MHz.

To transmit energy from an antenna the signal must see at least a ½ wave antenna. This can be made up of the Backstay on a sailboat plus the contribution from the antenna tuner plus the ground plain on the boat. The tuner has the task of making up the difference when the antenna and ground plain are to short or too long.
Zulu – another term for UTC or Greenwich mean time.

More Help!

- You can also follow our cruising adventure at our web page and find out where we are today at:
   http://sunnyside-adventure.webs.com
- If you need help send me an email at:
   p-t_on_sunyside@live.com
- Updates, files, and general information on this book and others:
   www.made-simplefor-cruisers.com

Come Join Us Living the Dream

Communication Log

Date	Call Sign	Frequency	Net	Comments

Index – Quick Reference Guide

"Handbooks for Starting the Dream" Series

Volume 1 – "Cruising Starting from Scratch"

Volume 2 – "Communications Made Simple for Cruisers"

Volume 3 – "Icom IC M802 Made Simple for Cruisers"

Volume 4 – "Radar Made Simple for Cruisers"

Volume 5 – "Icom IC M802 Starting from Scratch"

Volume 6 – "A New Ham I Am! Made Simple for Cruisers"

Get updates, free important downloads and other important Cruiser information at Made Simple for Cruisers:

WWW.Made-Simplefor-Cruisers.com

Discount Coupon for KISS-SSB Ground

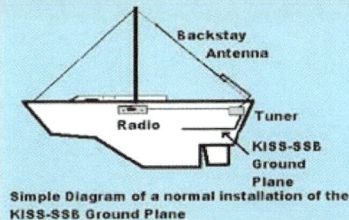

Made in the USA
Charleston, SC
12 June 2013